Venturing Into a Child's World

BY RICHARD D. DOBBINS

Your Spiritual and Emotional Power
Venturing Into A Child's World

Venturing Into a Child's World

Dr. Richard D. Dobbins

Fleming H. Revell Company
Old Tappan, New Jersey

Scripture quotations in this volume are from the King James Version.

Scripture quotations identified PHILLIPS are from The New Testament in Modern English Revised Edition—J. B. Phillips, translator. © J. B. Phillips 1958, 1960, 1972. Used by permission of Macmillan Publishing Co., Inc.

Scripture quotations marked TLB are taken from The Living Bible, copyright © 1971 by Tyndale House Publishers, Wheaton, Illinois. Used by permission.

Parts of this book previously appeared in The Leader's Guide to the videocassette series, *Venturing Into A Child's World,* © Copyright 1983 by Dr. Richard D. Dobbins.

Library of Congress Cataloging in Publication Data

Dobbins, Richard D.
    Venturing into a child's world.

    Bibliography: p.
    1. Parenting. 2. Child rearing. 3. Parenting—Religious aspects—Christianity. 4. Child rearing—Religious aspects—Christianity. I. Title.
HQ755.8.D62 1985   248.8′4   84-29842
ISBN 0-8007-1404-0

Acknowledgments

To my parents, my wife, my children, and my grandchildren, who have helped me learn practical arts of family living which cannot be acquired in the classroom.

Contents

———•••———

Preface

—•—

Raising children today is a real challenge. The pace of life is so rapid and parents' schedules are so crowded it is easy to lose touch with your children before you know it.

Still, there are many people who say to me, "Our parents and grandparents seemed to get along with their children all right. Why do we need more training for parenthood than they did?" The fact is, the world in their day was very different from our world. If they were living today, they would be confronted by the same challenges you face. Let me mention just a few ways in which their world was different:

1. *Their World Was Much Less Crowded.* Living in densely populated areas increases tension and anxiety. No one knows that better than you. For example, how frequently do you long to "get away"? More space and fewer people are more conducive to peace and tranquility.

2. *Their World Was Much Less Informed.* This doesn't mean that people today are any more intelligent or any wiser. However, there is no question about this being the most informed generation in history.

In fact, one of the unique risks of parenting today is in the influence the electronic media allow other people to have on your child. For example, he feels the impact of television very early in life—long before he starts to school.

In your parents' and grandparents' day the family was the dominating influence in a youngster's life until he entered junior high school. Today, your child is exposed to vastly different ideas about life as soon as he begins to listen to music and watch television.

3. *Their World Was Much Slower.* The speed of transportation and communication have so crowded parents' lives with choices that maintaining spiritual priorities in personal and family decision-making is much more difficult than in previous generations.

4. *Their World Was Much Simpler.* When life was more leisurely paced, parents and children were more likely to discover things about each other naturally in the course of living together. Today, with so much emphasis on doing your own thing, parents are torn between pursuing their own interests and providing their children with adequate parenting and a strong sense of family.

I have written this book to give you some practical guidelines, consistent with sound biblical teaching, to help you respond to the challenge of modern parenting with confidence that you can avoid some of its risks and enjoy many of its rewards. I hope you will find it helpful.

Richard D. Dobbins, Ph.D.

Venturing Into a Child's World

One
Venturing Into A Child's World

———————◆———————

Let's talk about some of the most valuable people in the world—your children. And, to keep this from becoming just another book about parenthood, let's look at the subject from a different perspective: the child's.

The miracle of your child's life begins to unfold at the moment of conception. A couple is never more like God than when in love they create life. Nothing else we do is as powerful.

Just think of it! As long as our children live they continue to draw energy for every expression of their lives from bodies which began as dynamic bits of matter no larger than the period at the end of this sentence. What about that for energy efficiency!

God Practices Family Planning

Whenever I talk about conception and birth, I am inevitably asked about contraception and birth control. People want to

13

know what the Bible teaches about birth control. Of course, there are no clear statements on the subject in the Bible. However, the Scriptures leave no doubt that God knows the value of family planning—and practices it.

The most carefully planned event in the history of the human race was the birth of God's "only begotten Son." Paul put it this way in Galatians 4:4,5: "But, when the fulness of the time was come, God sent forth his Son, made of a woman, made under the law, to redeem them that were under the law, that we might receive the adoption of sons."

All of God's children are planned. In Ephesians 1:4, Paul reminds us that God's children were chosen in Christ before the world was made. John tells us that everyone who is born into God's family is born by an act of God's will (John 1:13). In Revelation 13:8 and 17:8 we are told that our names were written in the "Lamb's Book of Life" before the world was created. That's family planning!

So, the principle of family planning is firmly established in Scripture. However, couples have both the freedom and responsibility for choosing how they will apply that principle in forming their own families.

Couples who take seriously their responsibility for family planning find themselves confronted with the question of birth control. Basically, there are four major methods of birth control: natural, mechanical, chemical, and surgical.

These can be viewed roughly on a continuum as illustrated below.

Least Risk to User   *Greatest Risk to User*

1. Natural   2. Mechanical   3. Chemical   4. Surgical

Greatest Risk of Pregnancy   *Least Risk of Pregnancy*

Each couple will want to make the particular method they select a matter of prayerful consideration since it involves their faith and philosophy of life. Your family physician will be glad to answer your questions about any method of birth control.

Knowing Mate Roles Helps You Learn Parent Roles

One of the greatest gifts you can give your child is an arrival which has resulted from this kind of prayerful planning and preparation. Of course, thoughtful couples will not want to undertake the roles of father and mother until they are comfortable being husband and wife.

In fact, learning how to be husband and wife should be the preliminary requirements for every couple who wants to be father and mother. Acquiring these skills usually takes from two to five years. Blessed is the child born to a couple who have learned how to be mates before they must know how to be parents.

Let Birth Be a Shared Experience

Few experiences of nature are as awesome to witness as the birth of a baby. Scripture suggests that God intends husband and wife to share this moment. Both the Old and the New Testaments begin with stories about families which are central to the message of Scripture. In Genesis we are introduced to Adam and Eve with their children. The Gospels focus on Joseph, Mary, and the divine conception of Jesus. In both of these families, birth was a shared experience. Adam and Eve were together when Cain was born, and Joseph was with Mary when Christ was born.

Modern approaches to childbirth allow couples to share this wonder. Your obstetrician's guidance is invaluable in determining which method will be most advisable for you. If he or she has a preference, it will be explained to you.

Healthy Priorities—Mate Before Child!

A child is the product of his parents' love for each other. In fact, that love is the source of his security. That is why healthy parents never allow their children to come between them.

Couples learn from Scripture that the relationship they have with each other is to be second only to the relationship they have with God. God told the woman that her desire should be to her husband (Genesis 3:16). He instructed man to leave his father and mother and "cleave unto his wife" (Genesis 2:24). In Matthew 19:6, Jesus says that, ideally, only death separates a husband and wife from each other.

One look at the natural order of life confirms the wisdom of this biblical counsel. Our parents usually die and leave us. And our children eventually grow up and go on their own. This exodus usually occurs during our forties and fifties. It is our marriage relationship that furnishes most of our meaning and security in the final third of our lives.

Parents Don't Have To Be Perfect—Just "Good Enough"!

Once you decide to have children, remember no one but God will do more to shape their destiny than you. The environment in which you raise your children will also make an important impact on them. Being aware of these factors should motivate you to learn as much as possible about parenting.

Of course, if you are willing to learn, your children will teach you more about parenting than you will ever discover in books. You can't beat on-the-job training! But usually you are in a better position to benefit from it if you know something about the job before you begin. That's where reading helps.

Remember, you don't have to be a perfect parent. Aren't you glad? Your child will grow up to be healthy and strong if you are simply "good enough." Now—most anyone can be a "good enough" parent, don't you agree?

Long ago, I learned there are no perfect parents or perfect children. It is reassuring to discover the average child can absorb all of the mistakes of the average parent without any lasting damage. Isn't that a relief!

You don't have to be a genius to be a successful parent. You don't have to be perfect. You simply have to be "good enough."

What Is a "Good Enough" Parent?

In case you are thinking, "I'm not sure I understand what being a 'good enough' parent really is," let me define it for you. The "good enough" parent consistently loves and disciplines in ways appropriate for the child.

Healthy love begins with the excitement of your child's conception. Most parents are in love with the idea of having a baby long before conception takes place. For them, learning that they will be parents is itself a cause to celebrate.

As the fetus grows, fantasies build around the idea of a child. When the baby is born, these fantasies are projected onto him. He becomes the embodiment of his parents' dreams.

Of course, not everyone is that excited about having a baby. Many couples haven't really planned or prayed for conception. In fact, learning they are going to be parents presents them with a dilemma. They don't want a child, yet they know one is on the way.

Even this kind of turmoil over a pregnancy doesn't have to keep a couple from being "good enough" parents. After all, God has given us nine months to fall in love with our unwanted surprise.

That's how it was with Fred and Esther. They had two boys: Dan, ten, and Don, eight. If you've been around boys this age, you know how challenging they can be. Fred and Esther loved their boys, but they didn't want any more children.

Fred was a hard worker with a good job. He and Esther had managed well and had just gotten to the place where the family could enjoy a few luxuries when Esther discovered she was pregnant again. They hadn't been careless. They had religiously followed their method of family planning, which made it even more difficult for them to accept this disappointment.

It was a shattering experience for them. They needed my help in managing it. When they first saw me, Esther cried, "Doc, I feel so guilty for thinking the things I'm thinking."

"To tell you the truth," Fred volunteered, "we don't want this baby. Esther is afraid of the delivery, and I don't know how we can afford it. Anyhow, it's not fair to our boys to force another child on them."

"How can we live with ourselves as Christians and think like this?" Esther sobbed.

If the truth were known, many couples find themselves in this dilemma. Fred and Esther worked hard at resolving it. I suggested childbirth classes and some parenthood training. We saw each other regularly throughout the pregnancy. They needed the full nine months to get ready for a task they didn't want to face, but they managed to fall in love with their surprise.

In reviewing some old case files, I found a note they wrote to me several months after their third little boy was born. It read: "How can we ever thank you for giving us a place where we could be honest about our feelings when we discovered David was on the way? At the time, we thought his birth was the worst thing that could happen. Now we wonder how our home could be complete without him. Even his brothers think he's great."

Tucked in with the note was a picture of a chubby, red-faced, adorable three-month-old baby boy—David.

Goals for the "Good Enough" Parent

In being a "good enough" parent you will need a limited number of practical goals. I am suggesting six. These goals are not difficult, but they will require you to get down into the world of your child long enough to teach him how to grow up into yours. Here they are:

1. *Help Your Child Feel at Home in His Body.* Few things are more important to good physical and mental health than your body attitudes. After all, it is through your body that you relate to your world. How do you feel about your body?

In Ephesians 5:28,29, Paul makes it very clear that it is God's will for a person to love his body. Parents are primarily responsible for teaching a child to love and care for his body as one of God's greatest gifts to him.

Sex education is an important part of our body attitudes. This essential preparation for life should take place in the home. Parents should be the primary sex educators of their children. In chapter 3, I will be giving special help to parents who want to talk to their children about sex in a way that is physically accurate, biblically sound, and mentally healthy.

2. *Help Your Child Discover His Personality.* Children are as unique as snowflakes. No two of them are alike. That's why Solomon has wisely advised, "Train up a child in the way *he* should go; and, when he is old, he will not depart from it" (Proverbs 22:6 italics added).

This ancient bit of psychological wisdom from God's Word is frequently misunderstood. Many assume it means there is one "right" way to bring up all children. And, if we bring up each child this way he will live like he should when he is an adult.

Others mistakenly think this promises parents who keep their children in Sunday school that their children will live for the Lord as adults. Sunday school and church attendance can be excellent influences in shaping character, but they are no guarantee of a child's spiritual future.

Actually, Solomon is saying there are as many "right" ways to bring up children as there are children. That is, each child is born with a unique disposition or nature. The "good enough" parent knows that and tunes in to it. He discovers the way in which each of his children needs to be trained and doesn't try to treat any two of them alike.

Any woman who has had more than one child knows that no two of them moved alike within her before their birth. Each had his own unique activity level. And, as soon as each is born he demonstrates his own way of interacting with his father and mother—unlike that of any of his brothers or sisters.

The child's personality is defined by his interaction with the personal and physical dimensions of his environment. Solomon's pronouncement underscores the tremendous importance of the child's early years in the development of his personality.

In chapter 4, I will be giving you some practical biblical guidelines for helping your child discover his unique personality.

3. *Help Your Child Become a Disciplined Person.* It is important for parents to understand the difference between discipline and punishment. Punishment is just one form of discipline. It involves inflicting physical and/or emotional pain for the purpose of eliminating undesirable behavior. Discipline is a much broader concept than this.

The confusion surrounding these two terms can be seen in a common reaction of adults to the misbehavior of an indulged child. They say, "My, that child isn't disciplined very well, is he? If he were mine, I'd give him more discipline."

A more accurate interpretation of their remarks might be, "My, that child isn't very well behaved, is he? If he were mine, I would punish him more."

However, even if you succeed in eliminating all of a child's *un*desirable behaviors, you still haven't helped him know what you consider *desirable* behaviors for him. So, if you are not careful, you can punish your child too much and discipline him too little. That is, he knows all too well what he is *not* supposed to do, but is unsure of what he *is* supposed to do.

Many Christians are like this. If you were to ask them what a Christian is supposed to do, they would respond by telling you all the things a Christian is *not* supposed to do. They think of their Christian life more as an avoidance of "the don'ts" than as an expression of "the dos." They are more oriented toward escaping punishment than they are toward gaining reward.

Punishment is a necessary part of child training. Children must learn that certain behaviors will not be tolerated. However, it is more important that a child be disciplined and taught what he *is* supposed to do.

Discipline involves learning how to invest your time, your energy, and your talent in behaviors and attitudes which are healthy and productive. A disciplined child not only has learned how *not to* behave; he has learned how *to* behave. In chapter 6 I will be talking about the three Fs of good discipline.

4. *Help Your Child Have a Healthy View of God.* Our views

of God are a very important part of our training for living. A child's self-concept is formed when he is between three and five. His ideas of God develop between five and seven. Healthy ideas about God serve as a sound mental health foundation. In chapter 8 I will be explaining how you can provide your child a healthy mental picture of God.

It is so easy for preschool youngsters to develop inaccurate ways of viewing God. Some of their views bring a chuckle. This reminds me of the little fellow who drew his mother a picture of his Sunday school lesson. You can imagine how surprised she was to discover he had drawn a garden with a road through it. On the road was a big black limousine. A chauffeur was at the wheel and a young couple in the back seat. Obviously puzzled by what she saw, the boy's mother inquired, "Johnny, what was your Sunday school lesson about?"

"Oh," Johnny replied, "it was about the Garden of Eden. You see," he said, pointing to the man in the front seat of the big black limousine, "this is God driving Adam and Eve out of the Garden."

5. *Help Your Child Learn Right From Wrong.* When your children are small, you can make most of their moral decisions for them. However, if they are going to be able to make the big moral decisions of life, parents must build into their children's consciences the tools necessary for that task.

Children need to learn the differences between *absolute* and *relative* moral issues. Some skills for this important task of discernment can be taught early in life. Others will have to await adolescence before the mind will be capable of grasping them. I will be explaining how to equip children for this vital task in chapter 9.

6. *Help Your Child Find God's Will for His Work.* It's exciting to see in each child's life the potential skills and talents for unique occupational expression. After all, there's nothing more thrilling than finding God's unique plan for your life. Your child deserves that opportunity.

This is one of the most neglected areas of parenting. As you will see in chapter 10, there are many ways in which you can motivate and challenge your child to discover his skills, develop them adequately, and pursue their application in a fulfilling and rewarding life.

Does this sound like a fascinating journey? Then, let's get started! As we venture into your child's world, our first challenge will be to help him *feel at home with his body.*

Two
Naked and Unashamed

———◆◆———

Each of us arrives here just as God created us–naked and unashamed (Genesis 2:25). For the first few years of our lives we seem to relish opportunities to frolic about without a stitch of clothes on. Obviously, we are born with healthy feelings about our bodies.

How long has it been since you watched a little baby celebrate momentary freedom from his diaper? Kicking excitedly, pulling his foot up toward his mouth, smiling from ear to ear, he is obviously enjoying himself. What parent or grandparent hasn't been delighted by such a sight?

Watching a youngster in a moment like that, you can't help wondering how he will feel about himself as he grows older. To a great extent, that will depend on what he is *taught*. If he is to feel good about his parents, about God, and life, he must be *taught* to feel that way. And he must first learn to feel good about his body.

In teaching your child to feel at home with his body you are making a major contribution to his physical, spiritual, emotional, and social health. His feelings toward himself will accompany him throughout life.

Of course, it is difficult to help your baby feel good about *his* body if you don't feel good about *yours*. First, then, let me ask you,

How Do You Feel About Your Body?

Remember, your body is God's gift to you. When God created us He made us body persons: "So God created man in his own image, in the image of God created he him; male and female created he them" (Genesis 1:27).

Often, when I ask a person how he feels about his body, I receive a vague reply: "I don't know. I've never thought about it."

Then I suggest, "If you don't know how you feel about your body, you can find out by taking a short and simple body-attitude test. The next time you bathe or shower, dry yourself in front of a full-length mirror. Take a good look at yourself and ask, 'How do I feel about what I see?' Then, while you are still looking at yourself, ask another very important question: 'What kind of care am I taking of my body?'

"If you have healthy attitudes toward your body, you will like what you see, and you will take good care of your body."

"Do You Love Your Teeth?"

I never will forget the time this little bit of common sense came crashing through to me. We had moved, and we had to find a new dentist. We were given the name of a man who had a very good reputation for being my favorite kind of dentist—a painless one. So, I made an appointment with him.

When I arrived in his office I was told that the doctor screened his patients through an interview process and there were no exceptions. So, I reluctantly filled out the necessary paperwork. When I finished it, he came into the room and began to ask me a series of questions. I never will forget how stunned I was when he asked me, "Do you love your teeth?"

I had never been asked that kind of a question before so I said, "What do you mean?"

"Do you love your teeth?" he insisted.

I paused, repeated the question under my breath, reflected upon it, and finally said, "Well, my teeth are a part of me and I feel good about me; so, yes, I do love my teeth."

"Good," the doctor replied. "Then I will take you as a patient. For we have found that people who do not love their teeth will not care for them. They make poor patients. However, people who love their teeth take good care of them. They are the people we want as patients."

We tend to care for whom we love and what we love. What kind of care do you give your body? Do you abuse it with chemicals? Food? Do you overwork your body? Do you see that it is properly exercised and rested?

On the following five-point scale how would you rate your feelings about your body?

1. Very poor
2. Poor
3. Neutral
4. Good
5. Very good

God wants you to love your body. It is His gift to you. Unfortunately, the institutional church has not always conveyed this impression. During a long period in its history the church portrayed the body as the enemy of the spirit. However, this is not taught in the Scriptures!

In the past, theologians have left people confused concerning the difference between the natural body and man's fallen nature. These are not the same!

Sarx *vs.* Soma

This confusion has been compounded further for Bible readers by translators who chose to use our English word *flesh* to represent these two very different Greek words. With few exceptions, when the Greek word *sarx* is used, New Testament authors are referring to the fallen Adamic nature—the "flesh." However, when the word *soma* is used, they are talking about the body. In most of our English translations, both words are at times translated *flesh*.

In Galatians 5:17 Paul warns, "The flesh lusteth against the Spirit, and the Spirit against the flesh. . . ." And in Romans 13:14 he exhorts, ". . . and make not provision for the flesh, to fulfill the lusts thereof." If you are not careful in your interpretation of these two passages you will conclude that the Holy Spirit and your body are in conflict. This leads to the false assumption that your body must be evil since it is the enemy of the Holy Spirit.

In both of these passages the Greek word translated *flesh* is *sarx*. However, you will get a clearer understanding of them if you read them this way, "The fallen nature of man lusts against the Spirit, and the Spirit against the fallen nature of man" (Galatians 5:17). "And make not provision for man's fallen nature to fulfill the lusts thereof" (Romans 13:14).

Reading these passages like this makes it obvious that it is not *your body* which is evil, but *the fallen nature of man*. You can see what a serious error in interpretation is made when a person concludes from these verses, or any other biblical passage, that the body is evil.

Such an error is brought sharply into focus by the admonition Paul gives husbands in Ephesians 5:28,29, "So ought men to love their wives as their own bodies. He that loveth his wife loveth himself. For no man ever yet hated his own flesh, but nourisheth and cherisheth it, even as the Lord the church."

The words *bodies* in verse 28 and *flesh* in verse 29 come from the same Greek word—*soma*. Here Paul uses a man's love for his body to teach him how to care for his wife. He is to love his wife as though she were his own body.

As you can see, the word translated *flesh* in Romans 13:14 and Galatians 5:17 is not the same as the word translated *flesh* in Ephesians 5:29. In Romans and Galatians, *sarx* is used, referring to man's fallen Adamic nature which tempts us to behave contradictory to the laws of God (Romans 8:1–8).

Obviously, in Ephesians, the word *flesh* is *soma,* which refers to the body.

The *sarx* we are to hate. It is our enemy! The *soma* we are to love. It is our friend!

Your Body Is God's Temple

Even a casual reading of 1 Corinthians 6:19 makes it very clear that your body is "the temple of the Holy Spirit"—God's gift to you as a Christian. Therefore, loving and caring for the gift of your body also becomes an important part of your Christian stewardship.

We are not taught to worship the body as an idol. But we are instructed to love and care for it as the sacred house within which we build our relationships with God and others to whom we are committed—family and friends. I will say more about this later.

Although your body may be marred or scarred by some birth anomaly, surgery, or accident, it's still the temple of the Holy Spirit. It may not be the most beautiful body in the world, but it's the only one you have, so take good care of it. After all, true and lasting beauty comes from within. It is that inner beauty which is closely related to your body attitudes.

Many physically beautiful women do not see themselves as being attractive. They believe they are ugly. Handsome men often suffer from the same delusion. In therapy I have suggested to such people that they are attractive. Inevitably, they disagree with me and think I am just saying that to make them feel better. On the other hand, we all have met physically unattractive people who are comfortable with themselves and seem to radiate inner beauty.

Body Attitudes Come From Parents

If you have healthy attitudes toward your body, thank your parents. One of the greatest gifts parents can give a child is a healthy view of his or her body.

As a parent, if you have unhealthy attitudes toward your own body, you certainly don't want to pass them on to your children. Ask your heavenly Father to help you change them. After all, He has fashioned and designed your body. You are someone very special to Him. When you were redeemed with Christ's blood (1 Peter 1:18,19) your body was included.

God affirmed the sanctity of the body when Christ was born. He reaffirmed it in raising Christ from the dead. God's insistence on raising all believers from the dead biblically substantiates the body as His good gift to His children.

Remember, our redemption is not complete until our body is raised from the dead (Romans 8:22,23; 1 Corinthians 15:51–58). If the body were evil, why would God raise it from the dead? Death would be God's way of delivering us from our wicked body.

When your heavenly Father views your body, He sees it as a treasure—something most valuable to Him. He has provided for its temporal care and secured it for eternity. He wants you, also, to value your body and take good care of it.

Body Attitudes vs. Sex Attitudes

Unhealthy body attitudes are often accompanied by unhealthy sex attitudes. Regardless of how your parents may have felt about sex, God is in favor of it. He not only chose to make you a body person, He also chose to make you a sexual person.

Genesis 1:27 makes it clear that when God created human beings He made them male and female. He didn't have to do that. He *chose* to do it. God looked at Adam and Eve; He saw them naked and unashamed (Genesis 2:25), and was pleased with what He saw.

God designed our bodies. He made sexual love to bond mates together in marriage. Sex is one of His wonders. Only Satan could turn something so beautiful and creative into something so wicked and destructive.

So the big question for parents becomes: How can we help our children avoid the temptation of selfish sexuality and its ugly consequences *before* marriage, yet still prepare them to enjoy a healthy expression of mature sexuality *within* marriage?

This task begins by doing everything we can to see that our youngsters have healthy bodies.

Excellent Medical Care Is Important

The thoughtful couple has gone a long way toward helping their baby feel at home in his body when they carefully select an obstetrician to supervise them during pregnancy and the birth process.

A wise way of going about this is to ask someone who knows the obstetricians in your community whom they would select to serve a member of their family. This allows the person to give you two or three names without having to comment unfavorably about anyone.

You may also find a similar approach helpful in selecting a pediatrician to begin caring for your child immediately after the baby is born. A thorough postnatal examination is extremely important to the well-being of your youngster. It is also very reassuring for the parents to know the baby has arrived physically healthy.

Allow Your Baby To Discover Himself

As soon as birth separates the baby from his mother he begins to define his own body boundaries. This is an amusing time. He finds his ears and pulls on them, sticks his finger up his nose, pokes himself in the eyes, and shoves his fist in his mouth. He engages in all of these entertaining activities while discovering what *is* part of him and what *is not* part of him.

Your own body attitudes will be tested when the baby extends his exploration to the territory between his navel and his knees. If you are not comfortable with your body, seeing how uninhibited your baby is may make you anxious and nervous.

As long as his toe is in his mouth or his finger is in his nose, his discoveries are cute—but when he starts to touch himself "down there" some parents get very uncomfortable.

I'm often asked, "What should I do when my baby fondles his genitals?" My standard answer is, "If the activity doesn't last longer than a few seconds, just ignore it. If it persists, then distract the youngster by changing his activity. If fondling occurs during diapering, simply pull a diaper over the genitals." Of course, what needs to be avoided is frowning at him, slapping his hands, or yelling at him.

Parents who are comfortable with their own bodies and their own sexuality will accept a normal amount of genital fondling as a routine part of the baby's definition of himself. After all, he is simply discovering what is "me" and what is "not me." This kind of exploration is as innocent as when he sticks his finger in his ear or rams his fist in his mouth. When you learn to see it like this, you can spare your baby the unnecessary emotional complications of your overreactions to such a normal activity.

Sexual Functioning Begins at Birth

God has designed sexual functioning to be a normal part of the infant's world. Shortly after birth a baby boy will erect and a baby girl will lubricate. These activities occur several times during sleep each night as long as we live. In view of this, it is easy to see how sexually stimulating the diapering process must be for the baby. We wipe the genitals with a warm, soft cloth. Then, we dry them with a soft towel. Once in a while we oil them. And, we pat them down with talcum powder.

Having been introduced to genital pleasure by the person who diapers him, you can understand how confusing it must be to the baby when that same person punishes him for trying to reproduce the pleasure for himself. From the child's point of view it appears to be all right for his parents to provide this pleasure for him in the diapering process, but it is not all right for him to discover it for himself later.

Such mixed signals can produce confusion in the child's

Baby Is Growing!

Simultaneously, a number of other things are happening in your baby's life. He is spending more time awake. During the day, he is awake an average of fifteen to twenty minutes for every hour he's asleep. He is smiling regularly. It is obvious he is enjoying life. He delights in your attention. Most of the time, he rewards his parents by sleeping through the night.

Also, by four months of age, your baby's legs will be strong enough for him to hold them in the air for long periods of time. If you compete with him to see who can hold their legs up longest, he will probably win.

When he is about six months old he will be sitting up. By then he will have enough control over the muscles which support his head and those which direct the movement of his eyes to be able to focus on a toy, pick it up, bang it any way he wants to, and pass it from one hand to the other.

About this same time your baby will discover how to put his thumb in his mouth. For some children this becomes quite a delicacy. However, the wise parent won't make a big issue out of it. Most children give up thumbsucking on their own when they are ready.

Of course, by now, he can also reach all other parts of his body. More than once, you will get a chuckle out of catching him with his toe in his mouth. And, since he can hold tightly to whatever he wants to keep, playing tug-o'-war becomes a favorite game for a while.

When he is nine or ten months old he will be crawling. He will also be able to pull himself up on his feet. At about one year of age your child can walk.

Home Will Never Be the Same

If you can imagine yourself paralyzed for months, and then suddenly being given the ability to move, you will have some idea of the urge your toddler feels to explore. Until now, the limits of his world, which have been determined by his caretakers, have gone unchallenged. Wherever they have put him determined what he saw, heard, and felt. Now that he can walk, he begins to challenge these limits which have been set for him.

Suddenly, your baby wants to see everything, feel everything, and taste everything. This is the time when you will want to make the house as accident-proof as possible.

Small valuable items should be placed out of the baby's reach. After all, forcing a child to restrict his actions in order to protect things you can easily move to safety infers that you value *them* more than you do *him*. Later, I'll have more to say about this when we talk about the formation of conscience.

Check the kitchen, bathrooms, and garage for anything that is poison. The risk of poisoning will never be higher for your child than between three and ten months of age. Hospitals report that 80 percent of all accidental poisonings of children occur at this age. A wise parent will keep a supply of syrup of ipecac on hand for emergencies.

Between eight and fourteen months of age your baby will baptize much of his world in milk, water, soft drinks, juices of various kinds, and any other liquid within his reach. This is the time for messes and spills. He is gaining more and more control of his arms, hands, and legs; but still, his coordination is not to be trusted.

Protect Your Child, But Let Him Explore

Electrical outlets and appliances, as well as machinery, are fascinating to toddlers. In safeguarding a child from these dangers, don't kill his urge to explore. Allow him to take reasonable risks. But protect him from the dangers he can't yet understand. Simple and inexpensive wall plug safety inserts will protect him from one hazard that is always at his eye level.

Crawling and climbing help him build confidence in his body. With your help, he will learn to avoid threats to his safety.

The overprotective parent who refuses to allow a youngster the excitement of reasonable risks often leaves him wondering about the sturdiness and reliability of his body. He becomes fearful of being hurt. He lacks the courage to discover how resilient his body really is. He is not comfortable with it.

Allowing your child to take a tumble once in a while helps him learn he is tough enough to take it. He finds his body is not brittle. It is not easily broken. He is comfortable with it. He develops a tolerance for pain and fear—refusing to let them deprive him of the joy and excitement of discovery. These are lessons he must master if he is to have the courage he needs to risk exploring his world.

"Sure, Dad. What Would You Like To Know?"

Many parents ask me when they should begin talking to their children about sex. They are surprised when I tell them sex education should begin as soon as the child is old enough to understand what he is told.

Such a statement would have overwhelmed the timid father who had finally braced himself to talk to his fourteen-year-old son about sex. "Son," he began bravely, "you and I need to have a little talk about . . . I mean, you are becoming a man now, and there are some things I need to tell you about. . . . Well," he finally managed to say, "we need to have a talk about sex."

"Sure, dad," his son replied. "What would you like to know?"

This story humorously illustrates the fallacy that sexual *ignorance* insures sexual *innocence*. Unfortunately, many parents still believe this. They assume that keeping silent about the subject of sex in the home will protect the innocence of their children and make it much more likely for them to enter marriage as virgins.

In a society as open as ours, nothing could be farther from the truth. The biblical ideal of premarital chastity is much more likely to be achieved by young people who have grown up with parents they could talk to about sex and sexual morality. After all, if you don't talk to your child about sex someone else will. That person is not likely to be as concerned about the sexual morality of your child as you are. So, why abdicate this opportunity and responsibility to them?

I believe that if many parents were given more practical help for educating their children about sex in age-appropriate ways, many would seize the opportunity.

By opening this subject with your child when he is learning about other aspects of his world, you make it easier for him to accept the information naturally, and grow up accustomed to talking openly and comfortably with you about the sexual issues of life. This secures for you the privilege of guiding your child in this sensitive and vital area.

Body Privacy

When your youngster is about two or three years of age it is time to begin teaching body privacy. Little boys should stop bathing with mother, and little girls should no longer bathe with father. Of course, dad and son may want to shower together; mom and daughter may want to bathe together.

If dad is not in the home to help bathe his sons, mom may have to continue to give the boys a bath. However, by the time they are four or five, boys should be able to bathe themselves.

Continuing to bathe with the parent of the opposite sex beyond the age of three risks overstimulating the child's imagination and sexual curiosity. However, bathing with the parent of the same sex helps youngsters satisfy their normal curiosity about how they are going to look when they grow up.

Some time ago I saw a delightful cartoon which beautifully illustrated this. A three-year-old girl was in the tub with her mother. The little girl's eyes were glued on her mother's body. It was obvious that she was fascinated by what she saw. Then, in an innocence that can only come from a child this age, she asked, "Mommy, how's come you's so fancy, and me's so plain?"

If it is possible, each child should have his own bed. In larger families, brothers or sisters may have to share a bedroom. However, bunk beds are not much more expensive than double beds, and they provide far more privacy.

When company stays overnight, it is healthier to let your child sleep in a sleeping bag on the floor than to put them in bed with someone else. There is no need to risk encouraging unhealthy sex play between peers, child molestation by an adult friend of the family, or incest. Incidentally, the greater statistical risk is from family members who sleep with children.

Even when your child is ill it is preferable for them to be cared for in their own bed. Some parents are tempted to bring a sick child into their bedroom during the night. There may be rare incidents when this is necessary. However, as a rule it is better for parents to make a trip or two into the child's bedroom to provide the necessary nighttime care, even though it may be more inconvenient for them. This maintains the parents' privacy and demonstrates their willingness to inconvenience themselves to give their child proper care.

By insisting on your privacy as parents, you are teaching your child to value his privacy. This adds to the respect he learns for his body.

If your two-year-old feels good about his body, he lets you know it. He begins to strut all over the house like he owns the place. You will want to reinforce these healthy attitudes toward his body by training him in good personal hygiene and teaching him the proper names of his genitals.

What To Call It!

Among the most frequently mentioned regrets of parents with whom I counsel is the fact of their failure to have open communication with their children about sex. In national surveys, only about 30 to 35 percent of children report having been able to talk openly to their parents about sex.

Most of us found it a forbidden topic in our homes. Our genitals were referred to as "it" or "down there." Sex education was limited to admonitions like, "Never touch yourself 'down there.' " And, "Never let anybody else touch you 'down there' either."

I believe parents should be their children's primary sex educators. I'm just as convinced that more parents would assume this responsiblity if they had some help with the what, when, and how of the process. There's no better time to start than when your youngster begins learning the names of people and things in his world. As vocabulary develops, labeling becomes a favorite game with children.

Why not take advantage of this opportunity to begin the important task of sex education? Since you will probably be toilet training your children during this time, it couldn't be more convenient. An ideal time to introduce the subject is when you are changing a diaper or giving your child a bath.

What Three-Year-Olds Need To Know

At this age, the goals are simple. Three-year-olds should be familiar with the proper names for their body parts. Little girls should know they have a vagina. Little boys should know they have a penis. They need to understand that this will never change. Accepting the permanency of their sex helps them begin to come to terms with the gender roles their culture expects them to assume.

Both parents should be able to talk freely about sex with their children. In later childhood, sons will probably be more comfortable discussing the subject with their father; and daughters will feel more relaxed when talking to mother about it. However, since mothers usually have more private moments with small children than dads, mom will probably draw this initial assignment.

Your conversation with your child might go something like this. "Honey, just as you have learned the names of all the other parts of your body, mother wants to teach you the names of your *genitals*. That is what we call the parts of us between our legs.

"Now, what did mother say we call the parts of ourselves between our legs? Gen-i-tals, that's right." Let your child practice this word several times. When you know he has the label properly learned, you can proceed.

"Little boys are different between their legs than little girls are. That is, little boys and little girls have different genitals. A little girl has a vagina. And, a little boy has a penis."

If you have children of both sexes in the family, you won't have to explain this further. Your child will have already made that observation. However, if your son or daughter has had no chance to see a child of the opposite sex without any clothes on, it will help illustrate what you are talking about if you have a drawing of a naked child to show him or her.

Continue to explain, "Mother is a woman. When she was born, her mother and daddy knew she was a little girl because she had a vagina. Daddy is a man. When he was born, his mother and daddy knew he was a little boy because he had a penis."

Some Things Will Never Change

Quite likely, your youngster will want to know if you still have a vagina and daddy still has a penis. Reassure them of this by saying something like, "Yes, mother still has a vagina, because she was born a little girl. And little girls have a vagina. They never grow a penis. Daddy still has a penis, because he was born a little boy. And little boys have a penis. Their penis never breaks off."

It may seem to you that this kind of reassurance is unnecessary, but when small children see each other without clothes on they observe the differences and make up their own explanations for them. In the magical world of the child, it is not unusual for little girls to assume that since little boys have a penis, eventually they will grow one. And, little boys may believe that girls also were born with a penis, but something happened to it. So, a small boy may conclude, something might happen to his.

This confusion was the subject of an adorable cartoon appropriately displayed in a pediatrician's office. It showed a little three-year-old girl and three-year-old boy facing each other as naked as the day they were born. Mother was getting ready to bathe them. The little girl was reaching for the little boy's penis. He was shouting, "Stop! Don't touch it! You broke yours off!"

Children Learn Words by Using Them

Don't be surprised when your children want to use these new words you have taught them. After all, they learn by practice. Naturally, in their innocence they may announce their discoveries at inappropriate times and places. However, this will be delightfully humorous to most adults. Those who have raised children will understand. Those who haven't will experience some of the delightful moments they would otherwise have missed.

You can imagine how embarrassed one mother we visited was when her darling little three-year-old daughter began to explain to my wife, "I have a *bagina*. And, you know what? Mommy's got a *bagina*, but daddy don't got no *bagina*. He's got a *penis*." Then, pointing to the design on the kitchen wallpaper, she revealed the significance of her discovery by concluding, "And, that's a flower!"

Now, she knew what to call "it." She had learned some new labels and was fixing them in her memory. Although our hostess' face turned several shades of red, my wife quickly commended her for taking the time to explain this important information to her daughter. Of course, that was an unforgettable moment for us.

Don't Forget To Explain the Plumbing!

These months when your child is building his vocabulary and compiling his own personal dictionary present you with an ideal time to explain his elimination functions to him. If he is not completely toilet trained, you may want to talk to him about this subject when you are changing his diaper. Bath time presents you with another convenient opportunity.

Simply say something like this. "My, honey, how big you are growing. Remember how little you used to be?"

After you have given him a chance to respond, continue with, "Do you know what makes you grow? God has made your body so that much of what you drink and eat is used to make you bigger. Then, what you don't need to help you grow, you get rid of when you go to the bathroom. Isn't that neat?

"You know, little boys and little girls both have a hole in their bottoms where stuff comes out. What comes out is the part of what you eat that is not good for you. The right name for that hole where the stuff comes out is *anus*. And the right name for the stuff that comes out of your anus is *feces*. It's OK for you to call it 'do-do' when you're little, but its real name is feces."

Then explain urination to them by saying something like, "There is a little hole in the end of a boy's penis and a girl's vagina that lets out the water we don't need to help us grow. Much of what we drink we need to help us grow, but what we don't need we get rid of when we go to the bathroom. That water is called *urine*. It sounds like 'you're in.' While you're little it's OK for you to call it 'pee-pee' if you want to, but its real name is urine.

"Feces and urine have a lot of germs in them. That's why we leave them in the toilet and flush them away. Once they are out of us, they are no longer good for us. That's why we get rid of them."

Such a thorough explanation may seem tedious and unnecessary to some, but parents who are willing to provide it will help satisfy the child's curiosity about his body, and make him more comfortable with it.

Insufficient information can create a lot of confusion in a child's mind. Here's a true story which illustrates this. A four-year-old boy, whose parents had carefully explained to him the genital differences between boys and girls, was in the bathroom using the toilet. He had locked the door.

His older sister had to go too, so she began pleading with him, "Sammy, hurry up. Please hurry. I've got to go so bad."

Little Sammy replied in a disgusted voice, "Oh, Susie, you know you don't got to go. You don't even got a penis!"

Incidentally, an extremely curious child may want to know the name of the little hole in the boy's penis and the girl's vagina from which urine flows. Of course, that is the *urethra* (pronounced—"you-ree-thra").

More Questions!

Having established this kind of openness in talking to your children about their bodies, you can be sure they will be back with more questions. Sooner or later, your four-year-old will ask, "Mommy, where did I come from?"

Then simply say, "You grew from a seed that was planted in a special room in mommy's tummy. When you were ready to come out, a door opened in mommy's tummy, and you were born."

A year or so later, the child may want to know how the seed got into that special room in mommy's tummy. Then, you tell him that daddy plants the seed there.

By the time your youngster is in first grade he needs to know that daddy plants the seed in mommy's tummy with his penis. Don't be surprised if the child wants to know how this happens. Usually, at this age, it is wise to respond by saying you will explain that more fully to him as he gets older.

It is important that the information you give the child is accurate. Your honesty is on the line. However, you don't need to feel obligated to give the child more information than he can emotionally manage.

The Preschooler's Favorite Game

Preschool children have three favorite games. They play house. They play school. And, when mother and dad aren't around, they play doctor. Sexual curiosity in childhood is at its peak during the preschool years. Most children will get involved in some kind of sexual play.

When you discover your child in sexual play, your reaction becomes extremely important in influencing his sexual attitudes. Here are some suggestions:

1. *Don't Panic.* Remember, this is something most every parent faces. You probably engaged in this kind of activity yourself when you were a child. You got through it without it ruining your life. So, don't panic when you discover your child in this situation.

2. *Calmly Break up the Activity.* If only your own children are involved, separate them and direct them into other activities. If other children are involved, send them home. Then, call their parents and inform them of what you found.

3. *Later, Have a Talk With Your Children.* After the anxiety of the moment has subsided, have a personal talk with your children. Explain to them, "Your genitals are the personal parts of your body. You are not to share these parts of your body with anyone until you get married. However, in marriage, God has designed a very beautiful way that a husband and wife can share their genitals in making love to each other.

"Until then, whether you are bathing your genitals, going to the bathroom, or caring for them in other ways, you do this when you are alone. This is why we sometimes refer to them as our 'privates.' "

At this same time, encourage your children to come to you if anyone, including members of the family, touches any part of their body in any way they should not be touched.

Notice the benefits of such a conversation with your child. Without traumatizing them, you have discouraged sexual play. In a very calm and deliberate way, you have told him genitals are not to be shared with playmates. You have also warned him about child molestation, incest, and homosexual risks. Still, you have presented genital love as something to look forward to in marriage. And you haven't loaded your child down with an unnecessary burden of masturbatory guilt.

Unbounding Energy

Once your child's initial burst of sexual curiosity is satisfied, he plunges himself into a world of almost endless activity. His kindergarten and early elementary years are filled with peers and play.

At times, getting him where he needs to be when he needs to be there will give you the feeling of being his personal taxi driver. However, during these years, he won't be bringing to you many deep and mysterious questions about the body or sex.

Children this age possess boundless energy. They like to express this in games of physical skill. Besides providing them a socially approved outlet for their energy, these games help them learn visual-motor skills and provide them the necessary exercise for building strong, healthy bodies.

Boys are likely to be interested in sports like baseball, football, basketball, and soccer. Girls may want to get involved in gymnastics, volleyball, softball, and swimming. As children become exposed to a wider variety of sports, their preferences may change. However, encouraging their involvement in physical games, consistent with their age and health restrictions, is a good investment in helping them learn wholesome body attitudes.

Personal Hygiene Is Important

Most of us can remember when we learned to bathe. After each bath, I had to present myself for inspection. If I had forgotten to wash between my toes, I had to go back into the bathroom and do it. That wasn't so bad. However, if I hadn't washed inside my ears, mother did it for me. I hated that.

If your little boy was not circumcised at birth, he will need to learn how to pull back the foreskin on his penis and wash away the smegma (a yeast-like substance which builds up under the foreskin). Your boy or girl should be able to bathe properly by the time he or she goes to school.

As early as possible, children should learn how to properly care for their teeth. Your dentist will have an effective way of teaching them, but you will have to supervise their practice.

Permanent teeth deserve daily flossing and brushing. Seeing that your child cares for his teeth this way will not only spare him pain and add to his general appearance; it will also save you money.

Grooming skills—shampooing, drying, and combing the hair—are usually the last to be learned by children. Of course, they are bigger problems for your daughter than for your son. Once these are mastered, your children have graduated from your school of personal grooming.

When your children appear well groomed, you have reason to be proud of them. However, you are entitled to an even greater sense of satisfaction if each child has learned to like himself as well as he likes his appearance. Your youngster will discover that being well groomed also makes it easier for other people to like him.

Spending the Night With Friends

In later childhood, years nine to eleven, your children will want to spend the night with their friends. They will also want to have their friends spend the night with them. It is important that you personally know the parents who will be supervising your child during his night away from home. You will want to be sure that their beliefs and values are similar to yours. It is risky to allow your child to spend a night in a home you have never visited, with parents you have never met.

If you cannot provide a separate bed for your child's overnight friend, then limit the number of times you permit him to have a friend over for the night. When you do allow it, be sure the children are well supervised.

Notice, I'm suggesting caution, not prohibition. Sleeping with a friend is a normal part of growing up. Nevertheless, with the risks that can occur in these critical years of a child's development, the wise parent is alert.

Privacy Without Prudishness

With all the care for privacy, it's important to avoid becoming prudish about the body. The rule is privacy, but not prudishness.

In a healthy family, children do not have to resort to pornography to satisfy their normal curiosity about what a nude adult of the same or opposite sex looks like. Neither is their sexual curiosity overstimulated by a parade of adult nudity through the house.

In a comfortable, open family, an occasional crack in the bedroom and bathroom doors when mom and dad are dressing reflects a healthy, casual privacy to the child. Even though children are not permitted to come in, or stand at the door and stare, there is no shriek of parental horror in response to them satisfying their curiosity by a passing glance.

In other words, try to keep your bedroom and bathroom from becoming like Grand Central Station, but don't guard them as though you were protecting the gold at Fort Knox. This kind of balance provides a casual environment which allows for the satisfaction of healthy curiosity, but avoids the risks of being overly permissive.

One More Preteen Talk About Sex

Before your daughter's eleventh birthday, and before your son's twelfth, you need to be sure they understand the process of reproduction and intercourse. Opening the subject again will also give you an opportunity to invite them to bring their sexual concerns to you when they are older.

From this time on, it will be better if dad talks to his sons, and mom talks to her daughters. Of course, if you are a single parent you will probably have to talk to both, unless there is another adult family member you can trust with the task.

To your daughter you might say something like, "Honey, it won't be long before you will be a young woman. What do you think about that?"

Give her a chance to respond. If she has any misgivings, talk with her about them. Then, begin again, "I know your health teacher will soon be talking to you about menstruation, conception, and childbirth. But you and I have always been able to share personal things, and I don't want our relationship to change that way, do you?

"Life is such a special gift from God; it is too wonderful to completely understand. And, at some time in our lives, most of us women experience the miracle of life growing in our bodies. Here's how it happens."

(At this point, show her a diagram of the female reproductive system. You can find a suitable one in a health book. If you do not have one at home, obtain one from the public library.)

"On either side of your tummy there is an ovary. (Indicate where the ovaries are by pointing to them on the diagram.) Every twenty-eight days, one of your ovaries will produce an ovum, or egg.

"Each ovum is about as big as a period at the end of a sentence. It will take two or three days for that ovum to travel through the fallopian tubes, uterus, and make its way out of the vagina." (Illustrate the route of the ovum as you talk.)

Then, take a diagram of the male reproductive system. Point to the scrotum and begin explaining. "This sac underneath the boy's penis is called a scrotum. In the scrotum are two oblong glands called testicles. (Point to the testicles.)

"When a boy reaches puberty, which is the time when he is capable of being a father, he will have millions of sperm cells stored in each of his testicles. When he is sexually stimulated, he reaches a peak in his excitement when those sperm cells spurt out of his penis. This is called 'ejaculation.'

"When a sperm from a man's body penetrates an ovum from a woman's body, she becomes pregnant. This means a fetus, which is what you call a baby before it's born, begins to grow in her uterus. In about nine months, the fetus finally gets big enough to live outside of her, and is ready to be born.

"God has designed a way to help a woman give birth to the baby. The muscles of her tummy get real strong and hard. The parts of her body which have kept the baby in her get softer, and she shoves the baby out through here. (Point to the cervix and birth canal.)

"What do you think about that?" Give her a chance to respond. Answer any questions she may ask. Then, continue, "Do you have any more questions?"

Reassure her, "Any time you do, honey, remember, you can always ask me. I want you to feel free to ask me anything you want to know about sex. God has made this to be such a beautiful part of our lives when we are married, I don't want anyone making it appear ugly to you. I want it to be something you look forward to enjoying when you are married to someone you love as much as I love your father."

You can use the same approach when talking to your son, by appropriately modifying the information. Such a conversation opens the way for later talks with your children about their adolescent sexual concerns.

Now let's turn from the subject of helping a child form healthy body attitudes, toward the exciting challenge of helping him discover his personality. In the next chapter, we'll take a look at some practical ways of applying Solomon's wisdom: "Train up a child in the way he should go; and, when he is old, he will not depart from it" (Proverbs 22:6).

Four
Introducing
Your Child to Himself

———◆———

Do you remember the first time you held a little newborn baby in your arms? What an awesome experience! The miracle of life is overwhelming. You are even more awestruck if the little baby happens to be yours.

Once you recover from the wonder of it all, you begin to realize how totally dependent he is on you. He arrives with no preconceived ideas, no prejudices. He doesn't know what or who you are. He doesn't even know what or who he is. He has no personality.

However, by the time he starts to school he will have definite ideas about you and himself. His personality will be evident to all who take time to get acquainted with him.

In the meantime, no one but God will have more to do with shaping that personality than you, his parent. That's quite an exciting challenge—helping your little person discover who he is. This discovery will grow out of his interaction with you, himself, other members of his family, his friends, and, when he is older, his Lord.

Principles of Parenthood

Your parents, or those who raised you, have been your primary source of training for parenthood. If they did a good job in preparing you for life, you have learned some valuable lessons in helping your own children get ready for their future. On the other hand, if you did not get this kind of help in your home, the responsibilities of parenthood probably overwhelm you at times.

It is regrettable that parents are provided so few opportunities to learn how to prepare their youngsters for life. Through contact with obstetricians and pediatricians, mothers learn the essentials in giving their children good physical health care. However, mothers get little help in providing for the emotional, social, and spiritual needs of their children.

Fathers are even more poorly prepared. In fact, most men know more about taking care of the family machinery than they do about caring for the emotional and spiritual needs of their children.

Family life becomes more enjoyable for parents who take the time to learn some basic principles of child rearing. It helps them to feel more competent in managing their children. In His dealings with us, our heavenly Father models three valuable principles of parenthood:

1. *God Creates Opportunities for Us . . . but We Decide How To Use Them.* In John 1:12 we are told, "But as many as received him, to them gave he power to become the sons of God, even to them that believe on his name." *Becoming is a process.* Beginning with our new birth, God gives us opportunities to *become—to develop ourselves—* as His children. But, He holds us responsible for choosing what to do with those opportunities.

Likewise, one of your most important functions as a parent is to create opportunities for your children to be healthy, educated, socially skilled, and spiritually alive. Your *children* will then have the responsibility for choosing what to do with those opportunities.

2. *God Sees Us as Unique Individuals.* He knows how different we are from one another. So, He treats no two of us alike. Our heavenly Father relates to each of us in ways consistent with our uniqueness.

Frequently, parents complain to me, "I don't understand why my son is having such a difficult time growing up. His brother and sisters are doing just fine. And I've raised them all alike."

Of course, these parents are well intentioned, but they don't know how impossible that task is. After all, personality is made up of the unique ways each child chooses to express himself in his behaviors, thoughts, and attitudes. So, no parent can treat all of his children alike. Even if it were possible, the children would perceive themselves as being treated very differently.

Just as each child has his own pattern of prenatal movement, he will have a unique personality. He won't be like anyone else. It is our privilege and responsibility, as parents, to help each child discover the unique person God has gifted him to be.

3. *God Loves and Disciplines Us as Individuals.* God gives to each of His children the love and limits that person requires. God deals uniquely with each. He treats no two of us alike; nevertheless, He is loving and fair with all. "For whom the Lord loveth he chasteneth . . ." (Hebrews 12:6). Notice: *Love comes before limits.*

Each child has his own language of love. It is your responsibility to learn it. Each has his own unique limits. You must discover them. Paul reinforces this pattern of love before limits for successful parenting: "Fathers, provoke not your children to wrath, but bring them up in the nurture and admonition of the Lord" (Ephesians 6:4). Notice that once again, nurture precedes admonition. *Love before limits.*

God's love prepares His children to accept His limits. Likewise, our children are better prepared to accept the limits we set for them once they are convinced of our love. It is the security of established parental love that enables the child to accept the restrictions of parental limits.

Let's see how these principles apply in helping your youngster discover his personality.

The Language of Feelings

The preverbal years—birth to two—are among the most important in shaping your child's personality. In fact, over 50 percent of what he will know by the time he is out of high school he will know before he can talk. The informal education you give your child at home will make more of an impact on him than his total formal education experience.

It will be two or three years before his vocabulary is large enough for him to have much to say to you verbally. However, long before then, the two of you will be communicating emotionally. Feelings are his initial language.

You can learn his new language better by seeing the world through his eyes. For example, you are very aware of birth as an adult experience. However, can you imagine what it was like for your baby?

Birth From the Inside Out!

Birth is a shocking experience for the baby. He leaves a world of darkness for a world of light. He moves from a crowded fluid environment within his mother into a spacious room of air. One moment his oxygen and food supplies are provided by his mother's body. The next moment, he is on his own. The temperature of his environment drops about 30° F. Before birth, he is in a world by himself; afterward, his room is filled with moving objects he will later recognize as people.

By seeing the birth experience from the baby's point of view, you will have a better understanding of his need for holding, touching, and stroking during those first few minutes and hours. After all, John (1 John 4:18) tells us that fear is overcome by love, and touching is the baby's language of love. In being nestled, cuddled, and warm he overcomes his fright at entering his new world, and learns to feel more secure and comfortable in it.

Finding a New Source of Food

About five days after he is born, the baby gets restless and cries more. Often, this is just about the time he goes home from the hospital. Although this move may be somewhat disturbing to him, the major issue is that the built-in food supply he was born with has been used up; so, he is feeling the pangs of hunger for the first time.

Over the next several months the parent-child relationship is going to be centered in the feeding process. Because we know our good intentions in caring for our young, it is hard for us to understand why our baby can't trust us to feed him. He will, in time. Our consistency will teach him. However, until then he will experience some anxiety.

When the baby first searches for food, a bottle or mother's breast is there. It's difficult for parents to understand how important that source of nourishment is to him. Remember, he has never had to search for food before. It was automatically delivered to him.

Of course, it's hard to improve on mother's milk, and it is so convenient. For these and other reasons, many women choose to nurse their babies for at least the first few months. Your pediatrician can give you good advice as to the nutritional and emotional advantages this may hold for you and your child.

During these early weeks and months of life, attachment between you and your child develops. This occurs within the context of several activities such as looking, feeling, gumming, and listening. While in your arms your baby experiences the full range of his emotions—crying, sucking, smiling, clinging, and cooing. When he is physically uncomfortable he resorts to rage.

One of the best ways to comfort your baby and stop his crying is to put him on your shoulder. In addition to the physical relief it brings, being held in this position exposes him to a different way of seeing the room, which stimulates his interest in what else is happening around him.

In time, your baby perceives you to be indispensable to his existence, so he internalizes your identity. That is, in the first six to eight months of his life he creates in his mind an image of you and his relationship with you. The emotional nature and strength of this bond plays a critical role in your future influence over the child's life.

Until this image is formed, it will be difficult for your youngster to tolerate being out of your sight while he is awake. He will be more comfortable and you will be more productive if you position him in the room where you are. An infant seat, playpen, high chair, or stroller can serve this purpose.

Ban the Bottle Holder!

Often, I have jokingly said the man who invented the bottle holder should be strung up by one. Some wire or plastic apparatus and a cold, lifeless mattress are no substitute for the reassuring presence of a mother's soft, warm breast.

However, bottle feeding your baby need not make any critical difference in him or your relationship with him. If he is held, cuddled, and has a chance to nestle against the warm body of a parent or other loving person while he is fed, he will get most of the emotional benefits of nursing. And, the formula his doctor prescribes will meet his nutritional needs.

Incidentally, have you noticed the posture of a little newborn baby as you hold him in your arms? It follows the contour of your body. You see, before birth, his posture was shaped by the internal contour of his mother's body. However, as he grows a little older and has more muscular control, he will raise his head, stiffen his back, and determine his own posture. This is how he begins to get a new perspective on his world.

Daddy Can Bottle Feed!

Bottle feeding has the advantage of allowing dad to participate in the feeding process. This provides him with a wonderful opportunity for body-to-body contact with his baby, which intensifies the youngster's attachment to him. It also permits him to give mother a little relief from those early morning feedings which are so inconvenient during the first few weeks of a baby's life.

Whether the child is being nursed or bottle-fed dad needs to be in touch with him. This is very important. Just as the baby learns to be comfortable with his mother's body, he also needs to be comfortable with his dad's.

The unique bond which forms from this close physical relationship between father and child can be the foundation of a close lifetime relationship. As a father shows this kind of love to his baby, he makes it easier for the child to respect parental authority as he grows up. Paul observes that the child who is nurtured by his father is more likely to respond well to his father's admonitions (Ephesians 6:4).

Babies Need the Masculine Touch

It is easy for any man to tell when a baby's daddy cuddles him enough. All he has to do is to reach out toward the baby as though he were intending to pick him up. If the baby has been in the arms of his dad often enough and long enough to feel comfortable there, he will spread a smile across his face and reach his hands out toward the man.

As a father, put this simple test to your baby. See if he will let one of your male friends pick him up. If he will, it's an indication you have taught him to be secure in your arms. If he won't, let that motivate you to hold him more. Of course, some youngsters, when they are about six months old, become very shy around strangers. However, this normal shyness shouldn't last longer than a few weeks.

Some single mothers are concerned about the fact that there is no father figure for their children in the home. However, there are ways to compensate for that. If she is living near her family, her father or brother can be encouraged to take a special interest in her children. If she is living at a distance from her family, becoming a part of a healthy, loving church can be helpful. There she can establish friendships with families who care enough about others to share their love with her and her children.

Also, pastors can be encouraged to have men on the staff in their church nurseries. Babies handled by fathers and grandfathers learn to be comfortable with adult males. Can you imagine what this does for the children of single mothers? Such substitute relationships can repair much of the hurt small children experience when their parents divorce. It can also give babies of two-parent families an important expansion of their social world.

First-Year Checkup!

Parenting is never simpler than during the first year. In fact, for the first eight months all that is required is physical care plus some love and attention. Nature does the rest!

Here are some of the things a "good enough" parent will want to provide for the newborn child:

1. A healthy diet.

2. Adequate health care under the periodic supervision of a reputable pediatrician.

3. Plenty of physical contact through feeding, bathing, cuddling, lifting, and touching.

4. A predictable environment—consistency and repetition help the baby feel comfortable and secure.

5. Appropriate toys.

6. Freedom to move about—consistent with his developmental and safety needs.

7. Verbal stimulation—even though the baby is not able to talk to you it is important for you to talk to him.

A World of Total Experience

Before your baby can talk he lives in a world of "total experience." He has no way to mediate his understanding of what he is experiencing. Let me explain.

It is his ability to talk that makes man unique among all living beings. Words are God's gifts to us for explaining life to ourselves. That is, if we use words in a healthy way they serve to increase life's pleasure and decrease life's pain. Talking to a friend about some painful experience through which we're passing brings us some relief. On the other hand, life's joys are multiplied when we share them with others. Our mental mood is markedly affected by how we choose to think—and talk—to ourselves.

Have you ever reflected on your thoughts while you are waiting to see the dentist? You hear some child cry. Then, you say to yourself, *I'm more experienced at this than that child. My dentist will be careful not to hurt me. It won't last long, anyway. And, just think how much better I'll feel and look when it's over.*

What are you doing with that kind of self-talk? You are mentally building your tolerance for an unpleasant experience. You are using your words to reduce your pain.

Words can also maximize our pleasure. After all, what's so exciting about four flabby pieces of flesh flapping against each other? Yet, isn't that what is happening when we kiss? The pleasure of that moment is maximized by what we are saying to ourselves during the process.

However, before a baby can talk there is no way for him to lessen his pain or add to his joys by the way he thinks about what is happening to him. As yet, he has no concept of time. He has no way of anticipating the future. When mother or dad says, "Wait a minute," he has no idea what that is. He lives in a world of *total experience.* He is in *total* pain or *total* pleasure.

Nestled there next to his mother or dad with a warm stream of milk coming out of the breast or bottle, he feels so good. He isn't mentally capable of comparing that pleasure with previous experiences, and he does not know it will end. That is why this is referred to as *total* pleasure—incomparable and unending.

On the other hand, he has no way of lessening his *pain,* nor can he anticipate *it* ending. If mother has accidentally left a safety pin open and it is pricking his skin, he doesn't have the ability to say to himself, "Wow, does this hurt. If mother knew the pin was sticking in me she would come and remove it so I would feel better." He is in *total* pain. He doesn't know it will ever stop.

More Pleasure Than Pain!

Once you understand this, you can appreciate why it is important that the youngster's preverbal years bring him *more pleasure than pain.*

From the time he is six to eight weeks old he should be regularly involved in activities which interest him. By the time your baby is ten to twelve weeks old he should be obviously enjoying himself some of the time and smiling regularly.

During these first few months, comfort the child when he is distressed. Usually, a pacifier will do the job. When it doesn't, hold him or rock him and sing to him. From about six months of age your baby can comfort himself much of the time by sucking his thumb, rocking, and playing with appropriate toys.

For the first seven to eight months of your baby's life, don't subject him to the pain of "crying it out." A baby this young can't be spoiled. When he can talk, that's another story.

On the other hand, it is impossible for a baby to have a life of total pleasure. And even if it were possible, it wouldn't be healthy for him. He needs to be prepared to live in the real world. Sooner or later, each of us has to get accustomed to some pain, but during the preverbal years of his life it is important that your baby experience more pleasure than pain.

Peekaboo and Pat-a-cake

At about eight months of age the child discovers that people and objects that he cannot see continue to exist. Often, we are made aware of his discovery by his ability to join with us in the game of peekaboo.

Typically, baby crawls over to the chair where dad is sitting. Dad is reading the newspaper. Baby reaches up and yanks on one of his shoestrings. Dad looks around the edge of the paper to see his baby staring at him with a wide-eyed smile on his face. Dad finds this amusing, so he smiles in return.

Dad goes back to reading his newspaper. Baby yanks on the shoestring again. This time, when dad looks around the edge of the newspaper and smiles, he says, "peekaboo." Dad and baby both smile and continue the game.

Dad is probably unaware of the reason for baby's smile. Baby is smiling because he has discovered that it isn't just dad's legs and torso in the chair. All of dad is there! And, when dad looks out from behind the paper, baby discovers that.

This important psychological discovery is called "object constancy"—a mental awareness that objects which have been seen continue to exist when out of sight. The dawning of this capability makes it possible for your baby to start building a picture of his world in his mind. This presents him with a powerful tool in learning to think.

At the same time, your baby is learning to use his hands more skillfully. He can bring them together in rhythm. This is demonstrated by his ability to play pat-a-cake.

These games provide some delightful moments for you and your child. You can enjoy them even more when you understand their significance in terms of your baby's mental growth and development.

The Roots of Language Appear

Between six and twelve months of age your baby begins to become self-aware. About this same time he will begin to form vowels and consonants into syllables. Talking to him will motivate him to babble back to you. Early indications of language learning come out of such interchanges.

These investments will be rewarded when the youngster is about nine or ten months old. That's the time you hear him say "Mama" or "Dada" for the first time. From then on, your baby will seek to imitate everything he hears you say. This results in some delightful bloopers.

Talking to your youngster during the diapering process, teaching him to identify his body parts, reading him bedtime stories—these are ways you can stimulate his verbal abilities. This kind of involvement will favorably affect the nature of his relationship with you. Incidentally, by the time he is fourteen months old you will have seen enough of his personality to indicate how well the two of you will get along.

Weaning

Weaning becomes more difficult if it is postponed much beyond the first year. Most children will wean themselves about this time.

Of course, a bedtime bottle may be necessary for several more months. And, if the family moves, another youngster is born, or some other significant family trauma occurs, your child may need the continued comfort of a bottle.

Be sensitive to the child's readiness for weaning. Don't make a major battle out of it. Try to excite the youngster with the opportunity to drink out of a cup like his older brother or sister and his parents.

Until a child is weaned, don't attempt to toilet train him. Attempting both of these tasks at once is overwhelming to him. However, once he is weaned, your child will be more receptive to toilet training.

"You Gotta Know When You Gotta Go"

It is wise to delay toilet training until your child is able to talk. If he has experienced more pleasure than pain in his preverbal world, he is now comfortable with himself and those around him. This provides a positive emotional environment within which he can learn how to control his elimination habits.

Four basic requirements for the child's success in toilet training are:

1. *Sphincter Control.* The sphincter muscles in the rectal area of the body control the opening and closing of the anus.

Remember, your child's brain gives him control over his body in predictable directions: from his head to his feet and from his spinal column to his finger tips.

It takes approximately two years for your baby's brain to give him control of the sphincter muscles. To expect your youngster to toilet train before he gains this control is really cruel. A parent making these demands prematurely doesn't mean to be cruel, but actually he is expecting the child to do something which is neurologically impossible for him at the time.

By delaying your efforts to toilet train your child until the later months of his second year both you and your child will be spared unnecessary frustration.

2. *The Ability To Talk.* He must be able to tell you when he needs to go to the bathroom. Most families develop their own private code words for their youngsters. Some common expressions are: "Gotta pee-pee." "Gotta do number one." "Gotta do a boo-boo." We were rather grandiose in our family. Our children would say, "Gotta make a river."

3. *The Ability to Anticipate.* He has to know when he has to go. His brain must be able to respond to the discomfort of a full bladder and bowel sufficiently in advance to give him time to make it to the bathroom.

When he is learning to anticipate, there are times when he doesn't quite make it. If mother and dad don't understand this, they may scold him for delaying too long. Even worse, they may assume that he is simply being stubborn and doesn't want to co-operate.

However, parental patience is rewarded as the youngster's brain gives him a little more notice. When he is able to anticipate his needs to eliminate far enough in advance, he will cooperate beautifully with you.

4. *The Desire.* Sometimes you can motivate a child's desire by encouraging little girls to imitate their mother's bathroom behavior and little boys to follow their father's example.

Potty prizes also help with some children. Keep some inexpensive toys or favorite desserts on hand. When your child succeeds in controlling his toilet habits give him his choice of potty prizes.

He's on His Way!

By the time your child is weaned and toilet trained, major parts of his personality are formed. How he responds to new tasks, the way he reacts to authority, the nature of his relationships with people—these are already obvious.

Before he is two, his life-style is obvious. That is, a trained observer can tell whether your child is more comfortable moving toward people, against people, or away from people. If he has learned to receive love from others and to respond to that love, the youngster generally moves toward people. If he has learned that people are a source of pain for him, and he is afraid of being hurt, he will be moving away from people most of the time. On the other hand, if he frequently experiences frustration in his relationship with adults, he may be seen already as moving against people.

Over the next two or three years, your child will internalize ideas about himself which he will carry with him through most of his life. This is what is referred to as his self-concept. I will define this more clearly for you in the next chapter and suggest some ways for you to be sure your youngster has healthy views of himself.

Five
Helping Your Child Find His Way

———◆———

Just as God relates to each of us in a way that is unique, and knows no two of us are designed alike, we should follow His example in raising our children. This is exactly what Solomon told the parents of his day. "Train up a child in the way he should go; and, when he is old, he will not depart from it" (Proverbs 22:6).

When I was growing up, my parents were given a different interpretation of that verse. In our church, well-intentioned enthusiasts felt Solomon was referring to formal religious training. They believed that Sunday school was such a powerful influence in a child's life that if you brought your child to church starting with his "cradle roll" days and kept him regularly attending until he was a young person, he would develop into a mature Christian. I'm sure that was not what the church intended to teach. At least, I hope it wasn't; but, that was the impression that came through to my family.

Your church and its Christian education programs are very important institutions for evangelism and training. However, your pastor will be the first to tell you that the church's success in training your child is dependent on your success in the family. The church and Sunday school can and should reinforce the home, but they seldom are able to override its influence, and can never replace it as God's designated child-raising institution.

Solomon's remarks are addressed to the family. By divine inspiration, he shares with his readers two observations about child rearing that, hundreds of years later, have been confirmed by psychologists. First, *each child is unique.* No two children are alike. Therefore, no two children can be trained alike. Second, *the roots of character develop in our early years.*

Introversive vs. Extroversive

The uniqueness of your child's personality begins to surface in his responses to weaning and toilet training. By the time he has accomplished these tasks you will have had a good look at his developing personality. What kind of a child is he? Is he quiet and reflective? Sensitive? These are qualities found in introversive people.

The more introversive person takes his reality into himself and reflects on it. Often, he has a rich and active fantasy life which prepares him to be a very creative person. He is likely to be a very private person who doesn't have great needs for being around other people.

On the other hand, an extroversive youngster is talkative and very active. He moves out and meets his reality, and is more openly social. His needs for people are obvious.

Neither is better than the other; just different. The extroversive child finds the same satisfaction in the rich relationships he forms with people that the more introversive youngster finds while reflecting on life in moments of solitude.

It is important for you to learn to *love your child as he is.* In frustrating moments, avoid the temptation to compare him with his brother or sister. When you and I were growing up we didn't like to hear our parents say, "Why can't you be more like your sister?" If you treat each child uniquely you will enjoy a much more satisfying relationship with all of your children.

Mom Is Always There!

Always try to be there when your child needs information or assistance. Although you should never let him use you to get his tasks done without involvement, as you answer the child's questions you are teaching him that other people can be called on when you don't have all the answers yourself.

By becoming excited about his projects you are showing him that others will share the joy of his accomplishments. He is also learning how valuable language is in enhancing his life.

During your child's second and third year, take time out to talk to him and read to him. From the time he has been able to say one or two words, he has been busy labeling, classifying, organizing, and filing away all kinds of verbal symbols representing everything in his world. His verbal interaction with you will help him immensely with this task.

It is very important for your child to master language before he starts to school. The more you talk to him, and the more you allow him to talk to you, the more likely it is that he will acquire the mastery he needs to achieve his potential.

This is an excellent time to teach a youngster that talking about troublesome things will help him feel better. In many homes, parents still believe that "children are to be seen and not heard." Today, many adults live in pain-filled silence because they learned this all too well when they were children.

This certainly was not the way Jesus felt about children. When His disciples tried to keep them away from Him, Jesus let them know that He was never too busy to talk to children (Mark 10:13–16).

Talking Helps

If a child learns that he can talk out his troubles with someone who loves him, when he becomes an adult he will be more likely to talk over his hurts with a friend. People who can do that are relieved of much of their anxiety and pain. Christian counselors encourage this. They help people talk about their hurtful experiences. They teach people practical, biblical ways of responding to their hurts so that the pain doesn't cost them God's best for their future.

However, many adults resist revealing their concerns to anyone because they have grown up believing this is a sign of weakness. Such inability to share one's burdens with a friend (Galatians 6:2) predisposes a person to needless mental health problems.

"Did You See That Crazy Idiot?"

In case you are unaware of how you reduce your own anxiety level by talking to others, notice what happens the next time you are with a car full of friends and some careless driver almost forces you off the road. After a scare like that, what is the likelihood that you will finish your trip without any of you mentioning it? I'll predict you won't go a tenth of a mile down the road until someone says something like, "Did you see that crazy idiot? He almost ran us off the road. We could have all been killed. Boy, was that close."

Then, if the threat was severe enough, someone else may say, "Whew! We almost got it. I don't know where that guy's head was. People like that shouldn't be allowed on the road."

And, when you reach your destination, one of the first things you'll say to people will probably be, "We almost didn't make it. Some dumb guy tried to run us off the road."

Why do you do this? There is no intellectual reason for such a rehearsal. Those who were riding together in the car all witnessed what happened. It is doubtful that any of them could add information the others didn't have. And why bother the people at your destination with this account? You *did* make it. That's obvious!

We hold this kind of conversation because it serves to reduce our anxiety level. That is its sole purpose, and a very useful one. Once the anxiety and fear have been drained out of the experience we can put it where it belongs—in the past.

Talking to God Helps, Too

Our children get acquainted with their parents on earth before they learn to know their Father in heaven. By encouraging our children to talk to us about their hurts we are preparing them for learning the advantages of prayer. After all, if they can talk to their earthly parents about anything, why should they be reluctant to share their concerns with their heavenly Father?

Unfortunately, if we are not careful, we unintentionally teach our children that they can only discuss with us the things we want to hear from them. They soon become expert in discerning what they can share with us and what they can't. If they get the impression that we love them only when they are pleasing us, then they hide from us any of their thoughts and behaviors they fear would meet with our disapproval. The more transparently our children can live with us, the more open they are likely to be in their relationship with God.

Unconditional Love

As soon as your child is old enough to understand, it is important for him to know that your love for him is not related to his behavior. That is, whether you approve of his behavior or disapprove of it, you love him just the same.

Your child will observe that some of his behavior brings you joy, but other things he does frustrate and anger you. He is likely to assume that you *love him* when you are *happy* with his behavior, but you *don't love him* when you are *angry* with his behavior.

You will probably need to explain to him more than once that you may feel one way about a *person* and another way about his *behavior*. The fact that you always love a person doesn't mean that you always love his behavior.

Explain to your child that your love for him is not affected by his behavior. There is nothing he can do that will make you love him any more. And, there is nothing he can do that will make you love him any less. *You love him.*

His behavior is a separate issue. When he obeys, you are very pleased with his behavior. At other times, when he disobeys, you are very *dis*pleased with his behavior. When his behavior pleases you, it makes you happy. When his behavior displeases you, it makes you angry. However, whether you are happy over his behavior that pleases you, or angry over his behavior which displeases you, *you love him just the same.* His behavior has nothing to do with your love for him.

I talk to many adults who have yet to discover this about their relationship with God. They believe His love for them fluctuates with the nature of their behavior. When their behavior pleases Him, they believe He loves them. However, when their behavior displeases Him they feel that He withdraws His love.

Unfortunately, this misconception of God's love usually has its roots in the way we felt about our parents' love when we were children. It is a tremendous relief for adults to discover that nothing they can do will make God love them any less, and nothing they can do will make God love them any more. He will never love them *less* than the love He expressed at Calvary and He can never love them *more.*

God may be pleased with our behavior or He may be displeased with our behavior. However, whether He is pleased or displeased, He loves us just the same. Discovering God's unconditional love frees us from the burden of trying to earn it, and motivates us to make our behavior more pleasing to Him. We seek to please Him because He *does* love us, not so that He *will.*

Children Need To Say Things Parents Don't Want To Hear

As early in his life as possible your child needs to know he can talk to you about anything—words he hears and doesn't understand, things he sees other people do that he is not allowed to do, his private fears he thinks other people may laugh at, or thoughts and feelings he has that you may not like.

A little four-year-old was not quite ready to share his parents with a new baby. So, when his mother and the baby came home from the hospital, he said to his father, "I wish Mommy had left the baby at the hospital." His dad wisely replied, "Yeah, it's tough to share Mommy, isn't it?" The little guy smiled and crawled up on his dad's lap.

A few weeks later, the four-year-old confided in his father, "I wish the baby was dead." Again, his dad proved a worthy confidant in saying, "I know. Sometimes little babies are a nuisance to big brothers, but you won't always feel like that."

When your child understands the unconditional nature of your love he will want to please you more and displease you less. The fact that he can talk to you about behavior he knows you don't approve of can help him deal with it more successfully. After all, he doesn't like that part of himself either. With your help, he can learn how to draw upon his strengths to overcome it.

Make It Easy for Your Child To Be Honest

Of course, few, if any, children are totally honest with their parents. Some of the funniest stories at family gatherings are the confessions of grown children to their parents. Secrets brothers and sisters have faithfully kept for years finally surface.

However, the child who feels forced to hide too much of his behavior from his parents eventually begins to hide it from himself. He denies it is a part of him. He blames it on others. He may also lie about it.

God encourages His children to be transparent. "If we walk in the light, as he is in the light, we have fellowship one with another, and the blood of Jesus Christ, his Son, cleanseth us from all sin" (1 John 1:7).

God warns us about being dishonest. "If we say that we have no sin, we deceive ourselves, and the truth is not in us" (1 John 1:8). And, He rewards us for being honest. "If we confess our sins, he is faithful and just to forgive us our sins, and to cleanse us from all unrighteousness" (1 John 1:9).

Make it easy for your children to be honest with you. Commend their honesty and reward it whenever you can. Should parents encourage tattling? If a child is honest about his misbehavior should punishment be altered? If so, to what degree? I will be dealing with questions like these in the chapter on helping your child learn right from wrong (Chapter 9).

Teach Your Child To Be Friendly

Find at least one family in your neighborhood or church with children the ages of your children. Make friends with them. Invite them into your home. This provides you the opportunity to teach your child some important social skills such as honoring others' wishes, complimenting friends, sharing, playing someone else's favorite game, and being kind to his friends and courteous to their parents.

If your youngster is in a good nursery school or day care center he will learn most of these skills. However, he needs to see them modeled by you at home, too.

Encouraging friendships which are obviously healthy is a very important part of parenting the preschooler. By showing an active concern about your child's friends then, you will be in a better position to influence their choice of friends later, in adolescence, when it is even more critical.

Healthy friendships help us develop positive aspects of our personality. The more positive your child feels about himself as a preschooler, the healthier his choice of friends is likely to be when he is a teenager.

Insist on knowing the parents of your child's friends. Get into their homes. Find out what kind of values they have. What interest do they take in their children? How closely do they supervise their children? How long are the children left unsupervised? Answers to these questions will tell you how much you want to encourage or discourage the friendships your child is forming.

When your child's friends are in your home, observe them. Are they wholesome in their approach to other people? Are they well mannered? Do they play fair?

It's Fun To Learn!

As the center of your child's life shifts from home to school, others will be more involved in helping your child discover and develop his personality. However, the challenge for you is far from over! Now, you will want to take an active interest in his school work.

Help your child discover he *can* learn, and that it is *fun* to learn. Be sure you place more emphasis on attitudes toward learning than you do on grades. Grades tend to fluctuate with the philosophy of the teacher's grading system and the motivation of the student. *In the educational process, healthy attitudes toward learning are more important than grades.*

Reward academic accomplishments with praise. Don't be the kind of parent who looks at a child's report card containing four A's and one B, only to say, "Why the B? If you could get A's in all these other areas, couldn't you get an A in this one?"

This is the kind of parent a child sees as very difficult to please. Your child will be emotionally healthier and his grade performance just as good if you praise his four A's.

"Cab Driver!"

Once your child is in elementary school he will become very active in the community. In fact, helping him get everywhere he needs to go will, at times, leave you feeling like a taxi driver. Special rehearsals for school events, activities at the church, team tryouts and practices—these are all "musts" on the social calendar of the elementary school child.

It is important that some member of your family be present at school and church performances when your child is participating. Although they may not be the most exciting times in *your* life, they are in *his*. When your child is standing up in front of the crowd and looking back through a sea of faces in the audience, you need to be there. Whenever possible, dad and mom should both be there to inspire the best in their youngster.

Parents Are Stewards of a Child's Opportunities

Helping your child discover his personality is an exciting challenge. It is an awesome responsibility. But in the final analysis, parents are not responsible for who their children become. No parent deserves all the credit or all the blame. We are only stewards of their early opportunities. *The ultimate responsibility must be the child's.*

It is your task and mine to tune in to each child's uniqueness and help him discover it. We are to provide a nurturant environment within which we first personalize our love for each child and then train him to discipline himself. In the next two chapters you will learn how to help your child become a disciplined person.

Six

Preparing Yourself To Be a Good Disciplinarian

———————•———————

Some time ago, while waiting for a plane at the Atlanta air terminal, I watched a mother struggle with two preschool boys. They looked to be about two and four years of age. If you've ever been around youngsters that age you know they have a thousand wiggles for every sit-still. As I observed the situation, it was obvious that this mother was being driven to distraction in trying to manage these highly active boys.

Every time the little guy would get too close to the big guy, he would get hit. And then the little guy would run to his mother, wailing and crying for comfort and protection. I watched that happen several times. Finally, the mother got so frustrated she said to the older child, "If you hit your little brother one more time I'll break your arms."

Of course, she was exaggerating. I hope her son knew that. As you can imagine, this warning from mother really endeared the little guy to his older brother. I watched the frustrated look on their mother's face, and thought, this dear lady needs some help in managing her children.

Before we leave this story, let me say a word to parents who are struggling with two preschool youngsters like this mother was. Don't underestimate the younger child's ability to get the older one into trouble. Somehow parents seem to be looking the other way when a little kid does or says something to antagonize an older one. However, just when the older child swings out in retaliation, mom or dad always seems to come on the scene. Only the transgression of the older youngster is seen.

Of course, mom or dad goes to the defense of the smaller child, lashing out at the older one, "Oh, you big brute! Aren't you ashamed of yourself? Picking on a little child like that!"

And all the time the little brother or sister is behind the parent making faces at the older child and saying, "Yeah! Yeah!"

Don't Confuse Punishment With Discipline

Most of us as parents need some help in managing situations like this. The mistake this mother was making there in the airport that day is one of the most common among parents. That is, we mistake punishment for discipline.

Paul talks about this in Ephesians 6:4, "And now a word to you parents. Don't keep on scolding and nagging your children, making them angry and resentful. Rather, bring them up with the loving discipline the Lord himself approves, with suggestions and godly advice" (TLB).

Punishment is only a small part of discipline. The primary purpose of *punishment* is to discourage undesirable behavior. On the other hand, the underlying purpose of *discipline* is to teach our children to use wisely the time, energy, and talents God gives them.

Life Is Built of Time, Energy, and Talents

Each of us has certain talents. No two of us are gifted alike. (Later in the book I will suggest some practical ways for helping your child discover his talents.) Each of us also has 168 hours a week—twenty-four hours a day. This is one way life treats everyone alike. None of us has one second more than another. And each of us has a limited amount of energy to use each day.

The way we use our time, how fully we develop our talents, and the projects we choose as investments of our energy— these basically define the kind of person we are. A disciplined person is one who uses these resources wisely in becoming the person he has the potential to be.

When our children are born, they do not have the knowledge, ability, or experience to control the use of these three life-building commodities. It is our responsibility as parents to furnish them with opportunities for learning to use these commodities wisely in building for themselves a meaningful, useful, satisfying, and happy life.

Don't be overwhelmed by this assignment. You don't have to be a genius to get it done. And, you don't have to get it done the first year your child is here. You have from eighteen to twenty years to accomplish this task. However, over this period of time the "good enough" parent will have gradually transferred to his son the responsibility he assumed for that child at the time of his birth. This is discipline at its best!

Biblical Methods of Discipline

Biblical methods of discipline include example, instruction, and intervention. Christ was a disciplinarian. In fact, those who followed Him and tried to put His teachings into practice were called *disciples.* Jesus used all three of these biblical methods in training His disciples.

First of all, Christ set before His disciples an *example* of His teachings. He demonstrated the life He wanted them to live. If you want disciplined children, then give them the model of a disciplined parent to emulate. Your children will be more likely to obey your directions if you give them an example to follow. Let them see what you are making of your life. It will challenge them to make the best of their own.

The power of example is amazing! A little three-year-old boy will walk like his father, try to talk like his father, and attempt to imitate what he sees his father doing. No wonder Paul used this method in training young Christians. Remember, he challenged them to follow him as their example (2 Thessalonians 3:7–9).

Second, Christ *instructed* His disciples. Every good disciplinarian is an instructor. Repetition is an essential part of any effective method of instruction. Parents often weary with telling their children the same things again and again. However, a certain amount of this is inevitable in the teaching process. When you are reading the Gospels, notice how many times Jesus repeats certain truths He wants to be sure His disciples learn.

Your Child Needs a Job Description

At each stage in your child's development remind yourself to give him a new job description. He needs to know what it takes to get your approval, not just how he can avoid your disapproval.

How would you like to report to a new job and not know what your boss expected of you? If you are like me, the first thing you would want is a good job description. That's what tells you how to please your boss. But, even more important, it lets you know when you are doing a good job.

Often in marriage counseling I ask, "Have you told your mate how to please you?" A common reply is,"No, but if he loved me wouldn't he know?" The obvious answer is no.

Mates are not mind readers. Many married people make the mistaken assumption that love mystically reveals to their mate what they need from them. If their mate hasn't had that revelation, they assume they are not loved. This is an unfair test of love!

Not until you have clearly told your mate the things which are important to you is it fair to assume that their refusal to provide them for you reflects a lack of love. It is much more likely that they simply do not understand what you want.

Poor communication of expectations is a leading cause of marital frustration. Your mate needs to know what you expect from him. Give him a job description!

If we need clear instructions from our mates, how much more do our children need them from us. We usually know what we want our children to do; so, we assume they know too—but they don't.

So, once you are sure your expectations are consistent with your children's capabilities, give them such a clear description of what you expect from them that they can repeat it back to you. Until then, try not to hold your children responsible for deliberately frustrating your expectations of them.

Of course, there are going to be times when children won't copy your example or listen to your instructions. Then we have to resort to the third biblical method of discipline: *intervention.*

When your child clearly understands what it takes to please you, and this is obviously something he *can* do, yet he deliberately chooses *not to* do it, then you must intervene in an appropriate way.

It is important to understand that at different ages different methods of intervention are called for. Also, remember that one child may respond better to a certain method of intervention than another. Suit the method to the child. Remember, Solomon said, "Train up a child in the way *he* should go; and, when he is old, he will not depart from it" (italics added).

Begin With a Predictable Schedule!

For the first six to eight months of your child's life the best discipline you can provide is a predictable routine and schedule. This often calls for an abrupt change in your social life. Before you have a baby you are free to enjoy an active night life. However, for the next few months you will have to sacrifice much of that for your baby's comfort. This shouldn't prove too disappointing since it provides you with an ideal time to become acquainted with your baby.

Now that you and your mate are parents, you will probably find yourself gradually moving away from childless couples and gravitating more toward couples with small children. Sometimes when a husband is not ready for this increase in responsibilities he unconsciously indicates that by preferring to continue socializing with couples who have no children. For several reasons this tends to put more stress on his wife. First of all, the physical demands of motherhood make it difficult for her to keep up the old social pace. Then, she usually is the one who makes arrangements for the babysitter. In addition, couples without children are usually not interested in talking about babies, which is a prime topic of conversation for new parents.

By changing the pace of your social life it will be possible for you to put your baby to sleep in his own bed at about the same time every day. This is important in keeping him on his schedule. As he grows accustomed to a predictable routine he is likely to have fewer gastrointestinal disturbances, sleep more soundly, and be more pleasant during his waking hours.

Easy Does It!

Until your baby is mobile don't even think about spanking. During this time, your primary training tools will be your facial expressions, the tone of your voice, and touch.

Smile at your baby when his behavior pleases you. Your smile has tremendous influence on him. That should come as no surprise. Look what an impact a smile makes on us as adults. Your smile communicates your love and approval to your baby.

A gentle loving touch also reinforces your approval. By patting him on the back you let him know you are pleased with what he is doing at the moment.

When you are displeased with your baby, frown and shake your head from side to side. Give him a firm tug on the shoulder. Say, "No!"–with a firm edge on your voice. That's about all your little fellow can absorb at this time. And, it's enough!

Mommy and Daddy Are Magic!

Remember, until your baby is approximately eight months old he has no way of understanding that things out of his sight continue to exist. During these months, it is better that you not be away from him for long periods of time. He can tolerate your absence for a few hours, but overnight absences and extended vacations should be delayed until your child is about eight months old.

During these early months your baby believes you are magic. He ascribes to you much more power than you really have. For example, when he sees you put a dish in the cupboard and close the door he believes the dish no longer exists. Since he can't see it, it no longer exists. From his point of view, you have made it disappear. Later when you turn off the vacuum cleaner and put it in the closet, he assumes you made that disappear, too. Since dad makes bigger things disappear, his magic is even more powerful!

You can imagine how frightening it must be to an infant when he feels one or the other of these powerful magicians is angry with him. For all he knows, in an angry moment they may decide to make *him* disappear.

How welcome the peekaboo period must be to the child. This occurs at about his eighth month. The smiles that he wears when he sees mother's and father's face emerge from behind a newspaper or book are the result of discovering that even when people he loves cannot be seen, they still continue to exist. They have not abandoned him. This discovery also helps him begin to attain a more reasonable estimate of his parents' power.

Looking back on our own childhood, it is obvious that we ascribed much greater power to our parents then they possessed. This underscores the importance of mom and dad giving their preverbal youngster enough physical contact to let him know their power is dedicated to loving him, not frightening him.

The Three Fs of Good Discipline!

Once your youngster starts to crawl and walk, it will be necessary to put limits on his freedom. In teaching him those limits you can begin using the "three Fs of good discipline." These guidelines will serve you throughout your years as a parent. So, learn them well.

1. *Be Fair.* Isn't that simple? Whether we're talking about the space allowed a toddler or the social limits imposed on a teenager, the principle is the same. *Be fair.*

"Good enough" parents are fair in their discipline. Youngsters can be damaged by parental favoritism. In families where such favoritism exists, children learn to play one parent against the other. This kind of prejudice can make brothers and sisters enemies for life.

No family is exempt from this possibility. It even happened in Isaac's family. The Bible says Isaac loved Esau and Rebekah loved Jacob (Genesis 25:28). This conflict began with Isaac and Ishmael, and is still reflected today between Jews and Arabs.

How can you be sure you are being fair? Compassion will help you. It is one of the major components of Christian character. The simplest way to experience compassion for your child is to imagine yourself in his place. Simply ask yourself, if you were the age of your child, how much freedom would be fair for you? How much could you manage? Putting yourself in the child's place helps you determine what is fair.

Of course, you will not be able to give a child all the freedom he wants. However, by putting yourself in his place you can more accurately judge how much he can be expected to manage responsibly. Children seem to have an innate sense of fairness. Even though they may find your limits restrictive, they will tolerate them better if they believe you are trying to be fair.

2. *Be Firm.* If you are being fair, then why not be firm? It is in the firm application of fair limits that a child gains much of his sense of trust. This is where many parents have difficulty. It's almost as though they equate being firm with being mean, and being lenient with being loving. Nothing could be farther from the truth.

Parents who both work outside the home seem to have an additional problem. Often they experience nagging guilt for choosing to work rather than be home with their children. Since they are not in the home during the day, they assume it is partly their fault when their children misbehave. So, even though such parents know they are being fair, they hesitate to be firm. They mistakenly attempt to compensate for their absence from the home by being lenient in their discipline. That is a great mistake. If your child is going to learn to discipline himself, he must learn to come to terms with limits.

Montessori day care center training can be very helpful in teaching a preschooler to become a disciplined person. Maria Montessori was a Catholic educator who believed that attitudes toward work are a major component of adult happiness. Her method of training involves introducing the child to age-appropriate tasks with various kinds of materials in a highly structured environment. These activities are not referred to as "play," but as "work." Children may "work" at such tasks as polishing silverware, cleaning vegetables, building with blocks, or pouring water from a pitcher into several glasses, and cleaning up their "work" area when they are done. The dignity and capabilities of the child are highly respected. Montessori children develop self-reliance, and also learn a healthy respect for the rights of others.

Mothers who work outside the home either due to their own choice or necessity need to know that once their child is weaned and toilet trained, there is no evidence that he will be harmed by being placed in a quality day care center.

Many working mothers I know make it a habit to occasionally stop in, unannounced, at the day care center their children attend. This affords them the opportunity of comparing actual practice with what the staff tells them about day-to-day operations. Also, without frightening your child, it is a wise precaution to remind him about the importance of privacy in caring for the personal parts of his body. Tell him to be sure to tell mom or dad if anyone tries to touch his private parts (refer to chapter 3, sections on *body privacy* and *the preschooler's favorite game*).

It is important that the day care facility you select be certified by the state, staffed by competent workers, and that it reflect the value system of your home and family. Many church-operated day care centers provide this kind of meaningful ministry to two-career families.

Of course, if a woman finds her fulfillment in mothering and the economy of the family does not require her to work outside the home, her children will have a luxury fewer and fewer families are able to enjoy—a full-time wife, mother, and homemaker. Homemaking is a noble profession!

Make it a practice to see that children get what they have been promised—good or bad. There are times when a child does wrong and needs to be punished. If you have promised him punishment, be sure he gets what you promised, provided it is fair and reasonable. At other times parents have promised a child a family activity, but when they come home from work they are so tired they can hardly push one foot in front of the other. So, they don't want to carry through on their promise to the child. It is important to the long-term interests of your relationship with your child that you muster the energy to keep your promise.

If we are to be successful parents, we must keep our word to our children. Disappointments should be rare, well justified and carefully explained. This creates an atmosphere of predictability, trust, and security that every home needs.

3. *Be Friendly.* Many parents find this characteristic of good discipline difficult to develop. It seems like we can't be firm unless we are angry. Why is it necessary to be angry in order to be firm? It is almost as though some parents mentally associate friendliness with permissiveness and firmness with anger. As long as they are friendly they can't be firm. And when they are firm they get angry.

Unfortunately, children learn that as long as their parent's voice sounds friendly they don't have to respond. Only when their parent's voice has reached a certain frantic pitch do they have to obey. Most parents don't like to yell at their children. Yet, through the years, their children have learned that they don't need to obey until mom or dad starts yelling.

Practice ways of being friendly *and* firm. The next time you are enforcing limits, why not say something like, "Well, honey, I know you're not very happy about our decision, but that's what we think is best for you this time. Now, you can cry and be miserable the rest of the day, or you can accept our judgment and get busy doing something else, but the decision is not going to change. I understand that you may not be happy with it, and that's all right. However, you know we love you and I'm sure you will respect our decision.''

From Principles to Practice

Through most of this chapter we have dealt with some important principles of discipline. These will be helpful throughout the parenting process—from the time your children are born until they leave home.

However, most of us need some specific techniques for dealing with youngsters of various ages. So, in the next chapter I will be talking about putting these principles into practice. Specific suggestions will be made for managing preverbal, preschool, and elementary school children.

Seven
Putting the Principles Into Practice

———————◆●◆———————

Good discipline rewards everyone in the family. It helps children gradually gain their freedom from their parents. And it helps parents gradually *regain* their freedom from their children. Young people are very open in discussing their desire to be free from their parents. However, it seems to be more difficult for some parents to admit the relief of knowing their children are grown and capable of taking care of themselves. Nevertheless, sometimes that reluctant admission surfaces in adult humor.

The story is told of a Catholic priest, a Protestant minister, and a Jewish rabbi arguing over when life begins. The priest insisted, "Life begins at conception." "Not so!" countered the minister, "Life begins when the unborn baby has a heartbeat." "You're both wrong," argued the rabbi good naturedly. Then, with a twinkle in his eye, he announced, "Life really begins when the last kid leaves home and the family dog dies."

After all, once you have a child neither you nor the child are free until you have helped him learn to successfully manage his own life. This usually means the responsibilities of parenthood are with us from eighteen to twenty years after each child is born. During this time the "good enough" parent gradually works himself out of a job by teaching each child to discipline his own life. The most valuable tool in this whole process is the child's conscience.

Help Your Child Develop a Healthy Conscience

God has made us to be moral. He has provided each of us a conscience, but the nature and content of that conscience are determined by our family and cultural environment.

For example, there are places in the world where children wear no clothes at all. Their parents wear very little. And they don't feel guilty about that because it is a part of their culture. In our country we would be arrested for appearing in public with so few clothes on. Other examples of the way culture influences conscience can be seen in our diets. In some parts of the world, dog is considered an edible meat, but cow is not. However, in our country just the opposite is true.

The nature of your child's conscience will grow out of his interaction with you and his perceptions of that interaction. You and I cannot control how a child chooses to interpret our interactions with him, but we can control the limits we place on his behavior and the way those limits are enforced. This is what determines how broad or narrow, rigid or flexible, hostile or friendly the child's conscience will be.

Remember, if you make the limits you set for your child fair, and enforce them in a firm and friendly way, you have gone a long way toward assuring him a healthy conscience. Your fairness gives him enough life space to make him comfortable, but not enough to overwhelm him. The firmness with which you enforce the limits set for him provides for his security—he knows where the boundaries are. And the friendly way you enforce the limits spares him from a harsh and angry conscience.

If this is the way your parents managed you, it is highly likely that you will manage your children this way. We do tend to carry over into our relationships with our children the child-raising patterns we observed and experienced while growing up in our own childhood homes.

If you feel your parents managed you in unhealthy ways, you will need to ask yourself some very important questions in order to avoid their mistakes. Here are some. What about my conscience is not healthy? Is it too narrow and harsh? Is it too rigid? Was I indulged? Do others find it difficult to tolerate me? Are my moral judgments sound? Am I able to discipline myself?

Define the changes necessary to provide your children healthy consciences. Pursue those changes diligently, but be careful not to overreact to your parents' mistakes.

In helping you to become more aware of the nature of your child's conscience and how you are shaping it, let's look at four general types of conscience: too narrow, too broad, unreliable, and healthy.

1. *The Too-Narrow Conscience* If you are an overly restrictive parent your child is likely to have a conscience that is too narrow. Often, this kind of parent is perceived by the child as enforcing very confining limits in harsh and angry ways. Scowling faces and screaming voices tend to frighten infants and small children.

Incidentally, most parents have never seen themselves scowling or heard themselves screaming. To give you some idea of what your child experiences when he is managed this way, the next time you are home alone, stand in front of a mirror. Then, reproduce the face you normally put on when you are correcting your child and say the same thing to your image in the mirror that you would say to your child—in the same way. If you were the age and size of your child, how do you think you would respond to such an approach to discipline? If you want a more realistic picture of what your child feels, tape record the whole experience. Then, as you look in the mirror, reproduce the facial expression and turn on the tape recorder. By listening to your voice while you look at your face you will see and hear something similar to what your child sees and hears.

Which parents are most likely to be overly strict with their infants and toddlers? Those who were raised by overly strict parents, parents who resented the time required to care for infants and small children—and parents who decorated their homes with expensive furnishings before their children were born.

Sometimes these parents will say, "I am not going to put any of my things out of our baby's reach. After all, every baby has to learn what he may touch and what he may not touch; so, he may as well learn it now." As you might expect, their baby is slapped and yelled at much more frequently than a child raised by parents who are wise enough to wait until he can respect valuable things before they acquire them.

As children grow older they find the *too-narrow* conscience increasingly difficult to tolerate. Much of the time their behavior is beyond the prescribed limits. Their disapproved behaviors are more frequently brought to their attention than are their approved behaviors. Consequently, they are prone to feel guilty and hostile much of the time.

These seeds of depression are likely to raise their ugly heads more often as these children get older. The way to avoid such an undesirable harvest in the lives of your children is to keep your approval within their reach. Make them work for it, but when they do, be sure they are aware of your approval.

Another type of conscience that spells trouble for your child is . . .

2. **The Too-Broad Conscience** A conscience that is too narrow makes it difficult for your child to stand *himself,* but a conscience that is too permissive makes it difficult for *other people* to stand your child. Of course, the obvious goal is to avoid both of these extremes. The wise parent will readily understand the child's need to be comfortable with himself and others.

Remember, the training for living received in the home will tend to generalize to situations outside the home. If you have allowed your child to strike people in his family or to destroy things in his home, he will tend to behave the same way in other social situations. Healthy parental love will not tolerate this kind of behavior.

3. *The Unreliable Conscience*   Parents who create this kind of conscience in their child usually punish him according to their moods rather than his behavior. If you let your child get away with almost anything when you are feeling good, but really clamp down on him when you are in a bad mood, you leave him confused as to where the limits really are on any given occasion. He will try to guess when you are going to be in a good mood so he can take advantage of you. He will also try to predict your bad moods so he can avoid your wrath. As you can see, in this environment the child does not learn how to manage his own life. He simply learns how to become a predictor of other people's moods so he can manipulate them and their circumstances to his advantage.

This kind of conscience predisposes a child to serious mental health problems in the future. Among the three kinds of unhealthy consciences we have talked about, this one is the most damaging.

4. *The Healthy Conscience*   A healthy conscience is characterized by limits which are clearly defined in the child's mind. He has not only been taught how to behave and how not to behave, but the reasons for these instructions have been thoroughly explained to him. The freedom given is enough to allow him to be comfortable with himself, but not enough to make others uncomfortable with him. The limits are consistently enforced. The child understands that it is his behavior and not his parents' mood that will determine his reward or punishment.

He knows that his mother and dad try to be sensitive to how he feels about life. The limits they set for him are not arbitrarily chosen from their memories of how their parents raised them, but are carefully defined out of their love for him. They are compassionate in both their definition and enforcement of those limits. They have made it clear that their love for him is not determined by his behavior. Regardless of how he behaves, they love him just the same. For that very reason, they discipline him. They want others to love him, too. They want his behavior to be gratifying to him and glorifying to God.

What Do You Do When You Make Mistakes?

At one time or another, most of us as parents have punished our child when he really didn't need it. So long as this happens only rarely, don't feel as though you have permanently damaged your child. Take comfort from my earlier statement—the average child is capable of absorbing all of the mistakes of the average parent without any lasting damage. You don't have to be perfect—just "good enough."

However, if you feel that you haven't been fair in the limits you have placed on your child or you have lost control of yourself and been much more severe with him than his behavior deserved, simply ask your child to forgive you. Children are very understanding and quick to forgive.

To neglect doing this is to risk serious damage to your relationship with your child. When you stop to think about it, an adult who punishes in anger is sending a child an obviously contradictory message, "As an adult, I am *out of control;* but I expect you, as a child, to be *in control.*" Can you imagine how confusing this must be to the child?

Often, when parents become Christians the Lord begins to deal with them about how they have managed their children. Ralph and Joan broke down and wept during a counseling session as I inquired into ways they had disciplined their children. They had two boys and a girl. Karl was six; Henry, thirteen; and Gloria, ten. They had forced these youngsters to wear clothes to school that would hide the bruises on their bodies.

"How could we have done that?" Joan sobbed. Through his tears Ralph observed, "And we thought we were right. I guess we did it to our kids because that's what our parents did to us." "What do we do now, Doc? How do we square things with our kids?" Joan asked.

I suggested, "Why don't you explain to them that since you have become Christians God has helped you to see a lot of mistakes you made as their parents. Ask them to forgive you. Then, let time prove to them that the Lord is making you healthier parents."

The family conference that followed provided Ralph and Joan an opportunity to share with their children some of the hardships they had faced while growing up. Their children responded to the apologies just as I had predicted. Now, both parents and children have more love and appreciation for each other. Their relationships are off to a new start in Christ.

Setting Limits for the Preverbal Years

For the first seven or eight months of your child's life there is no way you can spoil him. However, soon after that life begins to change rapidly for your baby. He becomes mobile—scooting, crawling, and standing with support. He begins to understand that things out of sight continue to exist. This intensifies his curiosity. So, setting limits and enforcing them become necessities.

The primary goal of disciplining babies is to protect them from physical danger. Sometimes the threat is from the environment, but at other times it is the baby's own impulsive behavior which threatens him. After all, your baby has no way of being aware of danger. In fact, it will be five or six *years* before he has *any* understanding of death. Until then, awakening in the mind a healthy fear of life-threatening situations is essential to his survival. This is done most effectively through carefully controlled physical punishment.

Pain—Pleasure—and Place!

God has designed your baby's brain to associate pleasure and pain with place. Therefore, it is important for you to apply this principle to teach your baby to avoid certain dangerous places and enjoy places reserved for pleasurable experiences.

Define the dangerous places in your baby's environment.

These will include areas around electrical outlets, open stair-wells, electrical appliances, driveways, and glass doors.

Select something that is thin, long, and highly flexible to use in spanking your baby. A thin plastic ruler is excellent. It makes enough noise to frighten the child, but does not inflict enough pain to harm him. Hold out the palm of your own hand and smack it with the ruler. This will help you to measure the amount of pain you inflict on your child. Never strike the child until you have sampled the amount of pain you intend to inflict on him. Only use as much pain as necessary to teach him to avoid dangerous places. Here is how you do it.

When he is playing in an area where he could be hurt, leave him there. Open his little hand and strike it across the palm with the plastic ruler. As you do this, look into your baby's eyes with a stern expression on your face and say, "No! No!" You can rely on his brain to associate the physical and emotional pain you are inflicting with the place he happens to be at the time. Then, pick your baby up and put him in a safe place to play. When you put him down, give him a favorite toy and smile at him. As you repeat this practice your baby will relate the rewarding toy and smile with the safety of the place you put him.

If he is a normal child, he will also crawl back to the same dangerous place immediately. Patiently repeat the whole process. Do this as often as is necessary for him to associate pain with the place you want him to avoid, and pleasure with the place where he can play with your permission.

Places of Pleasure and Pain

Keep your signals to the preverbal child as clear as possible. Avoid inflicting pain at places you want to be sources of pleasure. Protect the table, the bathroom, and his bedroom as places of pleasure for him. After all, you want him to enjoy eating, going to the bathroom, and sleeping.

If you spank your child at the table, on the toilet, or in his bed, you have made a place you want him to enjoy a source of pain for him. If this happens often enough the child may seek to avoid the very places you want him to enjoy. Often, parents who aren't aware of this behavioral principle can't understand why their child doesn't want to eat, won't toilet train, and resists going to bed.

Of course, it is inconvenient to take your child away from the table and out of the bed or bathroom to punish him. This requires discipline and control on the part of the parent. However, the results are worth it. Your child is less likely to resist the places you want him to enjoy. And, before long, simply mentioning the place where you take him for punishment is all that is necessary to bring compliance with your wishes.

Smack and Paintown

With a little imagination you can introduce very effective symbols of control to your child. Why not call your thin plastic ruler, "Smack"? Then, when your child is approaching a dangerous place, you can simply say, "Move away from the stairway, honey, or I'll have to get Smack, and you know what he does." It will amaze you to see how soon your preverbal child will understand what "Smack" is all about.

It also helps to have one designated place where you spank your child when it is necessary. The old-timers used the woodshed. In most cases, simply mentioning the woodshed got the results they wanted. We don't have woodsheds in our homes anymore, but there is no reason why we can't have a "Paintown." By selecting a special place to take your youngsters when they have to be spanked you are taking advantage of the brain's ability to associate pain with place. One or two trips to "Paintown" makes the mention of the place all that is necessary to gain the cooperation you want from your youngster.

Wean Your Child From Smack

As soon as your child begins to talk, involve him in the disciplinary process. Give him good reasons for the rules you ask him to keep. Explain why you want him to behave like you do.

Model the way you want him to live. After all, children learn most of their behavior skills through imitation and repetition.

Begin to replace physical punishment with more effective ways of helping your child manage his behavior. Here are a few you can use:

1. *Approval*   Your child will work harder for your approval than for anything else. Always keep it within his reach. Whenever he earns it give it to him. Even Jesus needed His Father's approval. And on more than one occasion, He got it (Matthew 3:17; 17:5).

See how often you can catch your children doing right. Every time you do, praise their behavior. Do not praise the child. It is too easy for him to confuse your praise with your love and assume you love him only when you are praising him. Focus your praise on the child's behavior. Say, "Oh, honey, you did such a fine job. I'm so proud of your work. You are really good at that."

2. *Withholding Approval*   Whether it is a picture that is not colored well, a kitchen task done less than excellently, or a mild display of selfishness, withholding your approval will often result in the youngster improving his next performance. When approval is not deserved and disapproval is not necessary this is often the most appropriate way to respond.

3. *Disapproval*   Be more generous with your approval than you are with your disapproval, but when your child misbehaves let him feel the sting of your disapproval. However, be sure to focus your disapproval on your child's behavior—not on him. If he feels you disapprove of him, he may conclude that you don't love him.

Imagine how it feels for your child to hear you say, "I am really disappointed in the way you treated your brother today. You are capable of doing so much better."

You may even want to let your child know that his behavior has angered you. "Mother has told you that you are not to touch the stove, but you did. You turned it on and burned up one of mother's good pans. I am so angry at what you did that I will need several minutes to decide your punishment."

Such a response lets the child know that you consider his misbehavior a serious thing. It keeps you from overreacting in a moment of impulse. And it models for him an appropriate way of managing anger.

4. *Threat of Disapproval*   Sometimes threatening your disapproval is all the deterrent you need to alter your youngster's behavior. Here are some examples:

"If you throw that, I am going to be very unhappy."

"Unless you can behave better for the next five minutes, I'm going to tell your father how disappointed I've been in the way you've acted today."

Just as your child desperately wants your approval, he also wants to avoid your disapproval. Warning him of impending disapproval while defining for him a way to escape can be a very effective disciplinary technique.

5. *Ignoring*   So long as your child's behavior is only mildly annoying it is advisable to ignore it. When you refuse to call any attention to the behavior it is highly likely your child will stop it.

Just the opposite also seems to be true. When parents notice certain behaviors they seem to worsen. Most children stutter while learning to talk. Many children suck their thumbs. Focusing attention on these behaviors tends to make them more difficult for the child to outgrow than if they were ignored.

Learn To Communicate With Your Child

Many parents have difficulty communicating with their small children. If you are going to succeed at the task you will need to develop some special communication skills. Begin by remembering that your child is not a mini-adult. Practice reflecting your child's feelings back to him. This lets him know you want to understand him. Here are some examples of how you might do this:

"My, you seem happy today. What has you feeling so good?"

"You're crying. Why do you feel so bad? Are you afraid I love your little brother more than you? Let's talk about it."

"I know it makes you angry that you can't go. We all get angry once in a while, but you will get over it. Until you do, why don't you get your pegboard and pound it?"

After you have accurately identified your child's feelings, let him talk to you about them. It helps for him to discover that you have feelings too. By demonstrating your willingness to be considerate of his feelings you are teaching him to respect yours.

Giving your youngster permission to think about how angry or hurt he is, and to talk about these feelings, enables him to develop healthy ways to manage his emotions while avoiding the painful consequences of acting them out.

Haim Ginott, author of *Between Parent and Child,* encouraged parents to stop any disruptive or destructive behavior and use the passive voice in explaining to their children why it would not be tolerated. At first you may feel awkward using the passive voice, but it is a very effective way to teach young children to deal with their feelings and behavior. If a child is striking a playmate, he should be stopped and told. "People are not for hitting. Balls are for hitting, but people are not for hitting." If a child tries to draw on the wall with crayons, you would stop her and say, "Walls are not for coloring. Coloring books are for coloring." Then you would help her find one.

Rewards and Penalties

Your child develops internal controls for his behavior when he is about five years old. This means his conscience is formed and functioning. It is time to wean him from "Smack" and control his behavior more through rewards and penalties.

Youngsters need to clearly understand what they will be rewarded for and what behavior their parents will not tolerate. One way of effectively communicating this to them is to make a traffic light out of construction paper and mount it on the inside of the child's bedroom door. Then, print five or six things the child is to do on a small piece of white paper and attach it to the green circle of the traffic light with rubber cement. In the same way, list two or three things that won't be tolerated and attach it to the red circle of the traffic light. Be sure to provide more ways for your child to be rewarded than for him to be penalized.

You may be able to find a more convenient or appropriate device than this, but the idea is to give each of your children a job description. Be sure they clearly understand the basis for rewards and penalties in the family. Then, follow through. Be fair! Be firm! Be friendly!

What About "Grounding"?

"Grounding," or confining a child to the home, may be an effective penalty for brief periods of time. However, once the time begins to accumulate, grounding becomes self-defeating. For example, once a youngster is grounded more than one weekend, he sees his confinement extended so far into the future that his hopes for freedom diminish, and the threat of more confinement loses much of its impact.

You may want to ground by the event. Here's how that would work. If your child deserves to be penalized, you might say to him, "All right, just one more time and I'm going to give you a grounding. Then, sometime when you want to go somewhere real bad, I'll collect my grounding and you won't be permitted to go."

Regardless of how you use grounding, you should make it possible for your children to work off their groundings by doing extra assignments around the house. This is consistent with the three Fs of good discipline.

As your children grow older the sophistication of your disciplinary techniques will have to match the level of their maturity. However, many of the principles defined in the last two chapters will continue to apply until they launch their own lives apart from the family.

In the next two chapters I will be dealing with the morality of your child's behavior. Until the early elementary years your morality has governed your child's behavior, but now he will begin to develop his own. The basis of that morality is his idea of God. This is formed between his fifth and seventh year. There are some steps you can take to insure that his concept of God will be healthy. We will discuss them in the next chapter.

Eight
Helping Your Child Have a Healthy View of God

———— •—•• ————

A Sunday school teacher asked her class, "Why do you children believe in God?" One little girl replied, "I guess it just runs in our family."

That's delightfully true. It's been that way from the beginning. Faith runs in families. We don't inherit faith; it's not genetic; but faith does have a way of becoming a family heritage—something passed from generation to generation. The God of Abraham becomes the God of Isaac; the God of Isaac becomes the God of Jacob; from father to son to grandson.

In some families mothers introduce faith to their children and to their children's children. This is how faith reached Timothy. Paul reminds him of that in 2 Timothy 1:5, "When I call to remembrance the unfeigned faith that is in thee, which dwelt first in thy grandmother, Lois, and thy mother, Eunice; and I am persuaded that in thee also."

Every child is born with the capacity to know God. However,

the family is responsible for developing this capacity. The concept of God you define for your child plays a major role in the purpose and meaning he attributes to life.

What Is Your God-Concept?

No one relates to God as He really is. We relate to Him as we picture Him in our minds. Your child's picture of God is a composite of impressions he receives from your family and your place of worship.

A small boy was busily sketching a picture with his crayons. Noticing the intensity of his effort, his mother inquired, "Son, what are you drawing?" Quick as a wink the little guy replied, "A picture of God." "Why, son, you can't be drawing a picture of God," his mother responded. "Nobody knows what He looks like." "I know, Momma," he said reassuringly, "but they will when I get done with this picture."

That picture may not have represented anyone else's view of God, but it was the way God looked to that child. Each child's view of God is unique. No two children see Him exactly alike, even when they are raised in the same family.

The view you have of yourself is referred to as your self-concept. The view you have of God is known as your God-concept. It is comprised of *a combination of mental images, feelings, and thoughts which give you your understanding of God.* Your God-concept is the lens through which you see God, and the lens through which you believe God sees you.

Where Do We Get Our Concept of God?

It might be interesting to see what you would draw if you were asked to symbolize God. It is important for you to be aware of the mental picture you have of Him, not only because of the powerful effect it has upon your responses to life, but also because it is likely to be communicated to your children.

Just as you give your child the view he has of himself, you

also give him the view he has of God. You have more influence on your child's view of God than any other person in his life. *Your child's God-concept comes from you!*

Why Is Your God-Concept So Important?

Your God-concept, the way you picture Him in your mind, determines your basic emotional attitude toward God. Whether you love Him, fear Him, or are angry with Him will depend on how you are viewing Him at the moment. The way you interpret daily events flows out of the nature of that relationship.

Any way you look at it, your view of God has an important bearing on your emotional life. If it is unhealthy it can frustrate your pleasures and increase your pain. If it is healthy it will lessen your agonies and intensify your joys.

Better or Bitter

None of us lives with the facts of his life. We live with a story we tell ourselves about those facts. Sooner or later, each of us has to learn how to deal with some very unpleasant facts in life—illness, career failure, family tragedy, bankruptcy, betrayal by a friend or lover, or divorce. The list is almost endless. The versions of the stories we could tell ourselves about the same set of unpleasant facts range from very destructive to very creative. Our view of God is a major determinant in which versions we choose. Consider the following.

Even with all of our medical advances, some parents still lose small children to diseases and accidents. Although the facts are amazingly similar in many cases, the ways parents choose to interpret the facts may be vastly different.

One couple may become bitter toward God, blame Him for not preventing their tragedy, and vow never to darken the door of the church again. Another couple might choose to believe their child is with the Lord, give their lives to Him, and determine to live so they will meet their child in heaven. Still another couple would accept the loss of their child as a tragedy from which there is no immunity, draw on the grace of their loving God, and survive their hurt to live again.

The nature of these interpretations is determined by each couple's view of God. The first couple see Him as punitive and harsh in His dealings with people. They respond in anger. The second couple see Him as compassionate toward people and allow Him to comfort them. The third couple see Him as their strength and determine they can survive anything with His help.

Are we talking about three gods? Of course not. There is only one God (Ephesians 4:6), but He is pictured in as many different ways as there are people who believe in Him. Even though they are probably unaware of it, these couples are reflecting their image of God to their remaining children.

Time for a Checkup!

How are you dealing with the unpleasant facts of your life? Most of us can manage the pleasant situations we face very well, but we need help in coming to terms with life's storms. Remember, there are almost unlimited versions of the story you could be telling yourself about any unpleasant facts you are facing. These interpretations would range from very constructive to very destructive. On the following continuum draw a circle around the slash mark which most nearly represents the destructiveness or constructiveness of the version you are choosing to believe.

Very destructive   **Very constructive**
/ /

Your children are acutely aware of your reactions to the storms of life. The pictures of God you reflect to them during these times are very important in shaping their own views of God. If you are having difficulty picturing Him positively in your circumstances, see your pastor or someone he recommends. Don't neglect yourself—or your children!

Helping your child build a healthy view of God prepares him to respond to all the events of his life—even the unpleasant ones—in the most constructive way possible.

Faith—Duty or Desire?

Whether your child eventually sees his faith as a duty or a desire will be determined largely by his God-concept. I'm sure you have seen your share of people who believe the Christian life is burdensome. They are like the lady who stood up to request prayer for herself by saying, "Pray for me in my weak way. Growing weaker every day. Pray that I may continue."

Where does such a view of the Christian life come from? It is the product of the way a person has been taught to see himself in relationship to God. Someone like this sees prayer, Bible reading, and church attendance as things you have to do if you are going to be a Christian. A healthy believer might see prayer as an opportunity to talk with God, Bible reading as a way to learn more about Him, and church attendance as a time to get better acquainted with His family. I would be among the first to say that the healthiest of Christians sometimes serves God because it is his duty. However, when your view of God is healthy, you serve Him most of the time because you desire to serve Him. You serve Him because you *want to,* not because you *have to.*

Fear or Love

If a child has a negative view of God he will fear life much of the time. John makes this clear in 1 John 4:18: "There is no fear in love, but perfect love casteth out fear, because fear hath torment. He that feareth is not made perfect in love."

Parents are not always aware of ideas children get in their heads about God. When your child is with you in an adult worship service, remember to ask yourself, "If I were my child's age, what kind of pictures of God would this meeting be creating in my mind?" If you feel the truths being talked about are overwhelming your child, discuss them with him on your way home or the following day. Be sure he understands them in a way that is consistent with the loving view God has of him.

This is a healthy practice regardless of the preacher's topic. You know what has been said in the meeting, but you don't know what your child has heard unless you give him a chance to talk to you about it. One of my favorite stories about how confusing church talk can be to children involves a preschool Sunday school class. The lesson was about the cross. When little Helen came home her mother asked her, "What did the teacher talk about today, honey?" "He told us all about his cross-eyed bear," she said. "He calls him 'Gladly.' "

"Are you sure that's what the lesson was about, darling?" mother questioned. "I'm sure, Momma, 'cause all he talked about the whole time was 'Gladly,' the cross-eyed bear" ("Gladly, the Cross I'd Bear")!

Tense or Relaxed

Your child's view of God can affect his physical health. It can mean the difference between feeling more tense or more relaxed in his approach to life. If he sees God as difficult to please, he is likely to conclude that God focuses more on one's faults and failures than he does on one's strengths and successes. However, if he believes God's yoke is easy and His burden is light, the child will see His focus as just the opposite. Talk to your child about his trips to church often enough to be sure he is hearing about the God you want him to know—a loving God who is our Friend throughout life. Make sure your child knows that Jesus not only wants him to go to heaven, but He also wants him to enjoy his trip!

Your Child's Feelings About God Are Important, Too!

It is not only important for you to know how your child believes God feels about him; you need to know how your child feels about God. Encourage him to love God, but be patient with him when he is angry with God. Let him know that God doesn't get angry with us just because we get angry with Him. He forgives us for our anger and keeps on loving us.

This experiential component of your child's spiritual development is very important. It is a dominant influence in shaping his attitudes toward God. Our attitudes are comprised of varying degrees of information and feeling. They predispose us to act predictably in our dealings with others. When you learn certain things about a person and have certain experiences with him, you form an attitude toward that person which motivates you to avoid him or seek to be with him. We certainly do not want our children to form an attitude toward God which would motivate them to avoid Him.

So, let's see that our children not only *learn about God,* but that they also *learn to know Him.* Remember, religious education and experience are more likely to be of permanent benefit to a person when they are introduced in developmentally appropriate ways. Such an approach is suggested in Paul's admission, "When I was a child, I spoke as a child, I understood as a child, I thought as a child; but when I became a man, I put away childish things" (1 Corinthians 13:11).

When Is Your Child's God-Concept Formed?

Your child's view of himself comes into focus when he is between three and five years of age. Of course, it includes impressions—thoughts and feelings which have accumulated in his mind since his birth. These have largely grown out of his interaction with his primary caretakers, who are usually his parents.

His view of God takes shape in much the same way. Initially, your baby believes you are omnipotent and omniscient. That is, he believes you can do anything, and you know everything. When he discovers there are things you don't know and things you can't do, it creates a crisis for him. Initially, this is resolved by adopting cultural heroes and projecting onto them his expectations of omnipotence and omniscience.

The Lone Ranger and Jesus

Several years ago, when the Lone Ranger was riding high in his second claim to fame, a Sunday school teacher was telling her kindergarten class about the crucifixion. As she dramatically explained how Judas betrayed Jesus and the Roman soldiers nailed Him to a cross, one little boy got so emotionally caught up in the story that he blurted out, "If the Lone Ranger had been there he'd have killed those dirty dogs and set Jesus free!"

For a time, a youngster believes his cultural heroes know everything and can do anything. However, when these prove to be no less human than his parents, the child finally reserves omnipotence and omniscience for God alone. At this stage in his mental and moral growth he begins to differentiate between God and man. Although it will be several years before he is able to picture God in any other than superhuman form, he is ready to develop his concept of God.

All of your child's impressions, thoughts, and feelings of a religious nature interact with his views of his parents to form his God-concept. This initially occurs between his fifth and seventh years. Like his self-concept, your child's views of God tend to be stable over time and highly resistant to change.

However, since his God-concept is formed later in his development it is more accessible to change than his self-concept. At times, I have been successful in helping a person change his self-concept by focusing first on his God-concept.

God-Concept vs. Self-Concept

Several years ago a woman came to me suffering from severe depression. I did not talk to her long before I discovered she had a horrible image of herself. She had carried these thoughts and feelings about herself all her life. They were reinforced by her frightening and judgmental view of God.

So I asked, "How do you picture God in your mind?"

106

"I've never particularly thought about that," she replied, "but I can tell you I'm very frightened of Him."

"What makes you frightened of Him?" I inquired.

"Well, I've been afraid of Him all my life—ever since I got saved," she said.

"Tell me about it," I insisted.

"As best I can recall," she began, "I was three years old when this evangelist came to our church and preached a sermon on hell. I was so scared when he finished that I ran to the altar like the world's greatest sinner and got saved. I can remember everybody making a fuss over me because I had gone to the altar. I know I was relieved at the time, but evidently it didn't make any lasting difference in the way I felt about myself. And I'm still scared of God."

Immediately I felt myself rebelling toward a religion that would put a load of guilt and fear like that on a three-year-old child. It wasn't just the one sermon this child heard, or that particular meeting, which I resented. Few children are so brittle as to be permanently affected by one such experience. It was a religious belief system that, in the remaining years of this woman's childhood and adolescence, reinforced, rather than corrected, her early punitive ideas of God.

Jesus felt the same way about adults who give children wrong ideas about God. Read Matthew 18:1–6. Jesus knew that when you turn a child's mind off to spiritual things you deprive him of life's most important discoveries—how much God loves him and how important he is to God.

Eventually I was able to help this lady correct her badly distorted God-concept. As she discovered God's love for her, she learned to love herself. I can't help but wonder how much of my work with her would have been unnecessary had she grown up in a home and church where she could have learned a healthy view of God.

You can't always control what takes place at church. However, you can see that your child's church experiences are interpreted for him in a spiritually healthy way. Begin to make this a practice as soon as your child is able to talk. Here are some guidelines to help you with this task.

Life's First Two Years

Swiss psychologist Jean Piaget refers to the first two years of life as the period of "sensorimotor intelligence." Although language and memory are apparent during the last few months of this period, there is no evidence of religious thinking. However, your baby develops religious-like behaviors in his relationship with you during this time that he will later transfer to God—behaviors such as trust, fear, comfort, joy, and awe.

During this time, you may teach your child to fold his hands and bow his head in prayer, but you should know that these activities are no more consciously religious for him than drinking from a cup or waving good-bye. However, he is keenly aware of any pleasantness or pain associated with religious activities. This brings up a very important question.

Is Church a Place of Pain or Pleasure for Your Baby?

If you want your child to enjoy church don't spank him there. If your church doesn't provide a pleasant nursery experience for its infants, and your baby is very active, then I would suggest you and your mate consider taking turns staying home with him unless you can afford a responsible babysitter.

You may be able to take him with you and force him to be still by spanking him, but such painful experiences will not make the kind of comfortable impression you want him to associate with his early memories of church. However, once he can talk and becomes more sociable, his desire to be around other children will make going to church a more pleasant experience for him.

Adult meetings have few, if any, positive effects upon the future faith of a baby under two. So, why should he be taken to church and spanked because he can't stay quiet for one or two hours? Why risk making his earliest memories of church such painful ones? After all, as he gets older, that's the last place in the world you want him to avoid!

Praise and Pleasure!

It is never too early to begin linking pleasure with religious activities in the mind of your child by smiling at him and praising him for religious words and gestures he repeats.

A few weeks ago I was conducting a seminar in a nationally prominent church. The pastor was a new grandfather and was revelling in the role. Of course, he wanted me to observe the spiritual vocabulary of his sixteen-month-old grandson. As the little guy rehearsed, "Jesus! Praise God! Hallelujah!" in baby talk, we all smiled and clapped. The baby doesn't have the vaguest idea about what those words mean, but he will repeat them again and again because he is rewarded with good feelings. Remember, his brain associates pain and pleasure with places, people, and experiences.

That's why it is important for your church to have a comfortable nursery department, staffed with *men and women* who love babies. When men are a part of the nursery team it is especially helpful to infants of single mothers whose babies miss the touch of their fathers. Each child should receive some special attention during the time they are in the nursery. Such a ministry begins to link the house of God with pleasure in a baby's mind.

Years Three and Four

During these years children experience their world with what Piaget refers to as "mythological artificialism." Life is like a giant fairy storyland to them. Clouds, storms, stars, and rivers are all made by some sort of divinely human effort.

For example, if you were to ask a child this age what makes the sun come up each morning, he might simply tell you, "God strikes a match and lights the sun." You can be sure he would say it with a straight face and a confident voice.

Preschoolers believe anything an adult says must be true. What a responsibility this places on parents and church leaders! It is cruel to take advantage of this beautiful innocence to teach children overpowering religious ideas largely designed to control them through fear and guilt.

At this age, your child is not mentally prepared for thoughts about hell, tribulation, and judgment. Premature attempts to introduce these concepts can be very damaging to his future attitudes toward spiritual things.

Does God Care Whether Children Eat Prunes?

Although it is never a good idea, a parent, in a weak moment, may resort to enlisting God's name to manipulate a child into obedience. I heard of a mother who stooped to such tactics in order to get her little preschool boy to eat his prunes.

Reasons for encouraging little boys to eat prunes are obvious to mothers, but they aren't always that obvious to little boys. This youngster must have had a good self-image, because he was able to counter mother's pressure with, "I'm not going to eat those prunes."

In utter desperation his mother shouted, "Son, don't you know God won't love you if you don't eat those prunes? God only loves little boys and girls who eat their prunes."

"I don't care if He doesn't love me," the little guy said, as he stiffened his resistance. "I'm still not going to eat those prunes."

So his mother said, "Okay, son, if that's the way you feel, then you get upstairs." Determinedly, he pushed his chair away from the table and stomped up the stairs with four little brown wrinkled-up symbols of resistance still in his dish on the table.

As the adults were finishing their meal, a huge cloud darkened the face of the sky. As a horrible electrical storm began thundering its way across the heavens, mother remembered what she had said to her son and was concerned about how he might be interpreting the situation. So, she decided to tiptoe up the stairs and peek into his room to see what he was doing.

As she cracked open his bedroom door, she saw her little boy with his nose pressed up against the glass of his window. He was looking up defiantly into the black sky, saying, "God, that's an awful big fuss to make over four little old wrinkled-up prunes."

What To Teach Preschoolers

Your preschooler is becoming acquainted with nature. This is an excellent time to teach him how God created the world. Reading an account of creation from a Bible story book might be a good place to start. Then, broaden this with stories about the sun, moon, stars, trees, grass, and weather.

Children love animal stories. The Bible is full of them. Genesis tells us God created the animals and allowed Adam to name them. Noah and the ark furnish you the material for many inspirational and instructive times with your youngster. Jonah and the whale make another exciting story, especially since it has such a happy ending. Think of the many times the Gospels mention fish and fishing. And, don't forget Jesus' stories about sheep and shepherds.

Children also like to hear about other children. Moses and the bulrushes, Samuel in the temple, baby Jesus, the lad who let Jesus feed a multitude with his lunch—these are just a few of the beautiful stories about children in the Bible.

Learning about God's world, discovering Jesus as God's way of showing how much He loves us, being taught how angels watch over little children—these are all wholesome aspects of the preschooler's religious education.

If Satan is introduced, he should not take on the form of a "boogey man" who "gets" bad little boys and girls who don't listen to their Sunday school teacher or mind their parents. Picture him as being under God's control. Reassure your child that God's love will protect him from Satan.

Productive believers are motivated to please God because they love Him, not because they fear Him. However, adults' irrational fears often have their roots in misconceptions of God stored distortedly in their memories since early childhood. Later in life, such twisted pictures of God often influence a person to see Him more as a punisher than a rewarder.

Years Five Through Seven

A five-year-old boy was trying to understand his great grandmother's death. His grandmother explained, "Honey, your
great grandmother is with Jesus."

"Can she see us, Grandma?" the little guy asked.

"Maybe," grandmother answered. "After all, God can see us,
can't He?"

The five-year-old thought for a moment, then, with a twinkle
in his eye, slanted his head to one side and said, while pointing
with his stubby little index finger, "If God can see us, He has to
be looking through that window right over there."

This story beautifully illustrates that children this age believe
God is all-powerful and controls everything; but, they still see
Him as human and magical. If you ask them to explain God to
you, something like this is what you are likely to hear: "God is
in the sky and you can't see Him. Sometimes He stops behind a
cloud to have something to eat. He goes down to land at night
and talks to shepherds."

This is an ideal time to teach children about prayer. They
have strong feelings about praying even though they still
largely see it as requesting material things from God.

During these years a child's view of the Bible is also somewhat magical. When you tell him God wrote the Bible, he pictures God with a pen in His hand busily writing. A little
kindergarten girl beautifully displays her limited view of spiritual things in this exchange: "I don't know much about God,"
she admitted. "You see, it tells all about Him in the Bible, but I
can't read yet."

Years Eight and Nine

Even at this age, children's thoughts are limited largely to
concrete situations. Piaget refers to their style of thought as
"technical artificialism." This kind of thinking joins a natural
explanation with an artificial solution. For example, when a

child is asked to explain the creation of the moon he might respond, "The moon is made of condensed clouds, but the clouds were made by God."

In his study, *Religious Thinking from Childhood to Adolescence,* Ronald Goldman found eight- and nine-year-olds picture angels as real people, wings and all. To them, God looks like a large man, dressed in a long flowing robe. They believe He makes frequent trips to earth, but lives in the sky. He appears angry and unpredictable. His voice is loud and powerful. Rarely do they see God as kind and loving. Often, they relate God's voice to restrictions and prohibitions—"Thou shalt not!"

Unfortunately, similarly distorted images of God are held by many adults I see in therapy. As you can imagine, your faith is not going to be very helpful in life if you see God as more judgmental than merciful, and more inhibiting than liberating.

Time To Clear Up Any Distortions

Eight- and nine-year-old children will accept whatever religious explanations are given them. This presents you with an ideal opportunity for correcting any distorted ideas of God your child may have. However, it is important for you to know how he is perceiving what you are telling him. The best way to be sure about this is to have him tell you in his own words what you have just said to him. Also, it may be interesting to have your child draw his impressions of God based on what you have told him. Either method will demonstrate clearly any remaining misunderstandings you need to clear up for him.

For children this age, *God* is likely to be seen as harsh and judgmental, while *Jesus* is seen as loving and kind. Since they also see God and Jesus as the same person, or mistake one for the other, it is important for you to be sure your child understands that both God and Jesus are loving and kind. In fact, that is why Jesus came to earth—so we would know what God is really like (John 14:7–10).

By this time, your child is capable of understanding that the Bible is a holy book either written by God or authorized by Him.

However, he is still not able to differentiate between the various divisions of literature in Scripture such as history, poetry, the major and minor prophetic books, the Gospels, and the Epistles.

Eight- and nine-year-olds love to pray, but their prayers are still quite materialistic and self-centered. They address their prayers to Jesus, but do not yet clearly understand that Jesus is a real person.

Great respect is given to all authority figures. However, the influence of parents is gradually diminishing while that of teachers is rising. Those in authority now have the opportunity and obligation to introduce children to more mature concepts of morality. So far these boys and girls have no real insight into what evil is. For them, being bad is simply breaking a rule. I will be giving you more specific helps in the moral training of your children in the next chapter.

Years Ten Through Twelve

At about age ten, many children develop a kind of dualistic view of life. Divine things are perceived as belonging to the magical world of long ago. Modern living is related to natural realms where God is not seen. However, as yet, they see neither opposition nor relationships between these worlds.

Since your child's understanding of God is more realistic at this time, the opportunity is ripe for you to help him see that any division we put between the sacred and secular is really artificial. If such a division is allowed to begin here a foundation will have been laid for the kind of unconscious duplicity which makes it difficult for many adults to see the relevance of Sunday worship to their everyday world.

During these years, it is extremely important for you to demonstrate and explain the practicality of Christianity to your youngster. Otherwise, as he grows older, he may reject sacred ideas as being impractical in his secular world.

Your child is now able to understand the multiple authorship of the Bible as being compatible with God's infallible inspiration of the Scriptures. So, this is an ideal time to talk to him about

how our Bible came to us. In case you have forgotten, you
take advantage of this opportunity to review and both you
your child will profit.

About this time, children begin to understand God as be
supernatural and not simply superhuman. However, they s
have difficulty grasping how it is possible for God to be at a
one particular place while He is also everywhere else at t
same time. A mature understanding of Jesus is also difficult f
them. Until about age thirteen, our child is likely to see Jesus
sort of a super magician.

In this chapter we have looked at the important role you
child's God-concept plays in his spiritual growth and develop
ment. The healthier his view of God, the brighter his spiritua
future. In the next chapter I will be showing you how to help
your child translate his healthy view of God into a wholesome
moral life.

Nine
Helping Your Child Learn Right From Wrong

———————•———————

Children growing up in the moral confusion of today's adult world do not always find it easy to know right from wrong. Can you imagine how embarrassed one proud father was the first time he took his little boy to the office? An employee asked him, "Son, how old are you?"

"Well," the boy replied, "that all depends on where I am. When I'm home I'm seven. But when I get on the bus, my daddy told me to tell the driver that I'm five."

Parental Consistency Is Important!

Often parents are unaware of the powerful impact such inconsistencies make on the moral character of their children. Your community and school environments are important influences in your child's life, but everything we have been able to

learn about character building indicates *parents,* and particularly *fathers*—not public officials, teachers, or ministers—have the greatest power in shaping children's values. *The home is the cradle of character.*

Behavioral scientists' discovery of the key role father plays in the development of his child's character should come as no surprise to Christian parents. Before the end of the first century Paul had identified dad as the primary source of nurture and discipline in the Christian family (Ephesians 6:4). In Colossians 3:21, J. B. Phillips quotes Paul this way, "Fathers, don't over-correct your children, or you will take all the heart out of them" (PHILLIPS).

Unfortunately, dads and moms get very little help in learning how to provide moral training for their children. Churches do a good job in helping us define our beliefs, but few practical suggestions are made for expressing them effectively in behavior. So, the sooner you realize that almost all of your child's moral training will come from you, the better you can prepare yourself to do the best possible job.

Begin by examining your responses to your own moral environment. How conscientious are you? Are you overly sensitive? Have you grown too permissive? What are your concerns? Do you share them with your family? Your child notices how you react to the faulty values of your culture. To not oppose them or, even worse, to accept them, is to morally fail your children.

What you think and how you feel about moral issues of your day can make a difference in the next generation if you share your convictions in meaningful ways with your children. For example, what would have happened to Moses and to Israel if Amram and Jochebed had been content to be just like the Egyptians? When it comes to teaching your children right from wrong, actions speak louder than words. Whatever you say you believe in on Sunday, do your best to practice the rest of the week. That is not always easy.

No one is more aware of this than the pastor. In a transparent moment, one minister lamented to another, "If you think practicing what you preach is tough, you should try preaching what you practice." Remember, our children know the difference between our talk and our walk. So let's do our best to present them with the consistency they deserve.

Now, let's take a look at the three most commonly used methods for teaching a child right from wrong:

1. *Moralizing* What is moralizing? It is telling children what they *should* and *should not* do. It is saying things like, "You know you should. . . ." "We just don't do things that way." "You know better than that." "How many times have I told you?" You might say it is preaching to your children.

This method works very well in teaching preschoolers and first and second graders right from wrong. They understand the moralizing parent is not pleased with their behavior. By using this method you can motivate your young child to try harder to gain your approval.

However, moralizing often backfires when you attempt to use it with older children. One of their favorite objections is that their friend's parents don't see things your way. Even when you get the compliance you want, the resentment moralizing breeds in the older child is easily seen.

2. *Manipulating* This consists of rewarding the child for doing what is right. "If you don't miss a Sunday in Sunday school this month I'll let you go to summer camp." "For every A you have on your final report card we will give you five dollars."

Manipulating often results in your child doing what you want him to do, but he has no deeper rationale for doing it than to get what he wants. His motivation is extrinsic rather than intrinsic—he is pleased with the reward rather than pleased with himself for having done something right and good.

As soon as he is old enough to be more rational in his moral judgments, give him good reasons for refraining from wrongdoing and doing what is right. There are bigger rewards than summer camp for those who develop the spiritual discipline of regular church attendance. Giving your studies your best effort pays bigger dividends than a dollar. As your child learns to feel better about himself for refraining from wrong and doing right, he will take more responsibility for his own behavior. What he says and does will be increasingly less reflective of your character and more typical of his. Gradually, his conscience will take over your function of parenting him.

3. *Modeling* Modeling is simply doing and saying in front of your child what you want him to do and say. This is, by far, the best method for helping him learn right from wrong. It makes an impact on children of all ages.

After a young man had publicly expressed his faith in Christ his pastor asked, "Son, what was it that I said in my message which caused you to accept Christ as your Savior?"

"I don't mean any offense, Pastor," the boy replied, "but nothing you said moved me to follow Christ. It is the way I've seen my dad and mom live."

First of all, model for your child the way you want him to live. Then, when he is small, use moralizing and manipulating as they seem appropriate. However, as he becomes more capable of understanding the rationale for the way you are teaching him to live, give him good reasons for his morality.

As early as possible, help him understand there is nothing which is good for him that he cannot enjoy. Assure him that when he wants to do things you will not permit, you will explain why they are not good for him. This probably won't take away all his desire to do those things. That's what temptation is all about. However, it will give him a good reason not to, and that's the stuff from which solid character is built.

Reward your youngster and/or praise him when he does what is right. Punish and/or penalize him when he does what is wrong. As he grows older, to show your pleasure with him use praise more often than reward. To show your displeasure, penalize him more than you punish him.

The Age of Moral Accountability

Theologians differ over how infants and young children relate to God. Some believe children are born innocent and need no other basis for their relationship with God until they are morally aware and have the ability to choose between good and evil. Others believe babies are born sinners and through infant baptism are protected by Christ's atonement. For others, infants are spared the consequences of their sinful nature through baptism or dedication, seen as symbolic events by which the faith of their parents is extended to them.

These are just some of the denominational differences over these basic philosophies and theologies regarding children. However, theologians agree that there is a time in each child's life when he becomes morally accountable for himself. Some religious groups have established twelve as the age for a person to assume this responsibility. Others allow the child to make his own declaration when he believes he has reached an age of accountability.

A child's mental abilities and the moral nature of his environment will affect the age at which he is capable of being morally responsible for himself. This means that some children may not be morally responsible for themselves until much later than twelve years of age. Others will reach this time in their lives much sooner.

Regardless of when your child reaches this time in his life, you will determine his readiness for it. That is why it is so important for you and your mate to be committed to the moral values you want to teach him. Your guidelines need to be clear and consistent. Your responses to his behavior need to be predictable. Praise and reward him whenever you can. Punish and penalize whenever you must. Be patient with him as he learns, but be sure he knows you hold him accountable for his behavior.

Now, let's talk about some character traits you can help your child build into his personality.

Life Is Valuable!

No child is born with an appreciation for life or a sense of danger. Once he becomes mobile, he would plunge down open stairwells, stick pins in electrical outlets, drink poison, shove his finger in an electric fan, or play in the street if you would let him. He has to learn to survive. In teaching your youngster to avoid certain high-risk activities, you are laying the foundation for helping him place a high value on life—his own.

When a new brother or sister comes along, teach the older one to be gentle with him or her. This won't be easy. After all, the baby is the newcomer, but he often gets more time with mom and dad. The apparent jealousy is hard for parents to understand. However, suppose your mate came home one day and announced to you, "Dear, I don't want you to get upset, but in a few months I am going to be bringing another mate into our family. There's no need for you to be jealous. Nobody will ever take your place. After all, I had you before I had anyone else." How comforting do you suppose those words would be?

Your child feels somewhat the same way when he has to share you with a new brother or sister. That's why it is not safe to leave the new baby with the older child until he has learned to accept him.

Some time ago I was visiting a young couple in the hospital who were celebrating the birth of a baby boy. Dad had brought their eight-year-old daughter and four-year-old son to see the baby for the first time. Their daughter could hardly wait, but the little boy wouldn't even go into his mother's room with his dad. When I asked him, "What do you think about your new little brother?" he stuck out his lower lip and said, "I wish we didn't got him."

However, as you reassure your older child that his share of love and attention has not been jeopardized by the newcomer, he will open his heart to his new little brother or sister. Until then, punish any efforts to harm the baby. But be sure to praise the older child when he is gentle and protective. By doing this you are teaching him to value a life other than his own.

When your child is old enough to be around other children, be prepared to intervene in any hair-pulling or biting. If he initiates it you will need to isolate him for three to five minutes. You may also want to spank him. However, remember the purpose of spanking is *not* to vent your anger at his behavior, but to inflict only enough pain to discourage it. When your child respects the safety of other children in play, praise him.

By praising him for being gentle with pets and punishing

him for any cruelty, you are helping him extend his respect for life to animals. Family pets are a healthy source of comfort for fretting children. Learning to care for animals teaches a child to be nurturant.

"It Is More Blessed To Give Than It Is To Receive"

A baby's world is very self-centered. In their second year they discover three favorite words: me, my, and mine. However, if you work at it, by the time the youngster is three, he can begin to learn the joy of sharing.

Some working parents feel very guilty for leaving their children in a day care center. Often they attempt to compensate for this by buying them special gifts. If you tend to do this, teach your child to share those gifts with his friends. Otherwise, they will simply make him more selfish. Explain to your child how long you had to work in order to buy what you gave him. Let him know his gift represents a part of you. This will help him learn to value what you give him and to take care of it. Show him where to store his toys and make him responsible for them. Such training will usually help him to be careful with his friends' things.

A generous character is not spontaneously born. It emerges through years of sharing and giving. Teaching your child to be generous is not easy, but it will pay big dividends in his future relationships with his family and friends. Selfish people are shunned by their friends and resented by their families. They are often lonely, bored, and frustrated. Helping your child learn to share will go a long way toward protecting him from such unnecessary misery and securing for him the love and respect of his family and friends.

Cooperation Is the Name of the Game!

Just as children tend to be selfish rather than generous, they also tend to compete rather than cooperate. This is first seen in sibling rivalry—competition among brothers and sisters for parental love and attention. Here are some things you can do to minimize sibling rivalry.

First, give each child some special time with you. This may test your ingenuity, but you can do it. Second, don't compare one child with another. This is a form of manipulation that is sure to backfire. When you say, "Why can't you be good like your brother?" what are you teaching a child about himself? What kind of feelings are you promoting between your children? Third, reward your children for cooperating with you and with each other. Once a child is two, he can be trained to cooperate in a common task. I admit, this requires patience.

It's easier to put a child's toys away than it is to teach him to put them away. It's easier to clean up a child's mess than it is to teach the child to clean up his own mess. However, if you take the easy way your child doesn't acquire the skills he needs for common tasks around the house and you wind up taking care of him long after he should be able to care for himself.

If you can be patient enough to allow your children to learn household tasks, then you can teach them to cooperate with each other. With younger children you can begin by having them pick up things with you—toys, clothes, papers, leaves. Show them where you want the things put. Older children can learn more complex tasks—setting the table, doing the dishes, running the vacuum, dusting the furniture, making beds, carrying out the garbage, mowing the grass, washing and drying clothes. Let them do these things with you or for you.

Promise them a group reward when their tasks are done—a trip to the store, hamburger stand, swimming pool or maybe the amusement park. Of course, the nature of the reward should be related to the size of the task. Be sure you don't praise one child for doing more than the other. Limit your praise to the group.

While you are teaching cooperation you are also teaching fairness. This is why it is so important that you distribute responsibilities as equitably as is reasonably possible. Children seem to have an innate sense of fairness. If one child thinks he is being asked to do more than the others, he will complain. You need to determine whether his complaints are for his own convenience or are legitimate matters of fact.

Respect for Older People

Teach your children to respect older members of the family for what they have contributed to the family's well being. Learning that they have their grandparents to thank for giving them their parents, aunts, uncles, and cousins helps youngsters see their grandparents as special people. Unless you tell them sooner, it will be years before they figure all these things out for themselves.

In caring families, children learn that, out of respect, older people are served first at mealtime. I was helping myself to some meat at a friend's house when their little five-year-old daughter was anxious to serve me another dish. "Dick, would you like some potatoes?" she asked. You can imagine how embarrassed my hostess was.

However, my friends felt free to call me by my first name, so their daughter saw no reason why she shouldn't. This was her time to learn. So, her mother explained to her, "Honey, children never call older people by their first name, even if they are your friends. Because your daddy and I are older we can call our friends by their first name. When you get older you can, too, but for now you call this man Dr. Dobbins."

Without a moment's hesitation, the darling little girl said, "OK, Mommy." Then she turned to me and asked, "Doctor Dobbins, would you like some potatoes?" Doing favors like this for older people is another way children have of showing their respect.

I Cannot Tell a Lie!

Our national legend about George Washington and the cherry tree underscores the emphasis most American parents place on honesty. However, it is difficult to know when a child can differentiate between fantasy and reality with sufficient clarity to be held strictly accountable for telling the "truth."

This observation is beautifully illustrated in the following story. A four-year-old girl came running to her mother yelling, "Oh, Mommy, come quick. There's a bear in the back yard!"

Of course, that kind of news brought mother to the kitchen window on the double. What she saw was not a bear, but a big sheep dog. "Doris, that is not a bear," mother protested. "It is just a big dog. Now, honey, you're old enough to learn not to lie. You must always tell mother the truth. So, I want you to go upstairs, kneel down by your bed, and ask God to forgive you for lying to mother."

In a few minutes Doris came bounding down the steps. Her mother intercepted her before she could get outdoors and asked, "Well, Doris, did you ask God to forgive you for lying to mother?"

"Yes, ma'am," the little girl replied. "And He said, 'That's OK, Doris. The first time I looked at it I thought it was a bear, too!' " With that, she rushed out to play. Fortunately, her mother understood her intentions were not to lie. The little lady was learning to live with a very active fantasy.

You can encourage honesty in your child by rewarding it. When you must punish or penalize him for doing something he has been honest enough to tell you about, be sure he understands the consequences would have been more severe if he had lied.

However, don't force him to confess what you have seen him do. Once in a while, I meet parents who apply their own cruel lie detector test. They see their child hit his brother or sister. Then they say, "Come here! Did you hit your sister?"

The child knows he's going to get spanked; so, in a desperate effort to escape it he says, "No, Daddy. I didn't hit her."

"Don't you lie to me, boy. If there's anything I can't stand it's a liar. Now, did you hit her, son?"

There's no excuse for putting a child through a third degree like this in the name of teaching him to tell the truth. When you see your child do something for which he needs to be punished, you have all the evidence you need. Act on it. Don't further intimidate the child by making him condemn himself or be called a liar by his parents.

What About Those Bad Words?

Once your child starts to mingle with other children in the neighborhood you should be prepared for the new words he is likely to bring home. Many parents are so embarrassed when asked to explain their meaning that they simply say, "That's a bad word and I don't ever want to hear you say it again."

Your child deserves a better answer than that. After all, these words are not equally bad. Some are worse than others and some are rather innocent. He needs to know the difference.

All "bad" words can be divided into four categories: slang, vulgarity, profanity, and blasphemy. These range from the more innocent to the more evil. To help you see this more clearly let me picture them on a continuum for you.

More Innocent			More Evil
Slang	Vulgarity	Profanity	Blasphemy

Slang involves words like: gosh, golly, darn, foot, shucks, nerd, phooey. Many families develop their own unique slang words. These are often used to express surprise, disgust, or frustration. When your child wants to know the meaning of some slang word you may want to respond by saying, "Son, that's a slang word and most slang words don't have specific meanings. They are just expressions of surprise, disgust, or frustration."

There is no clear biblical restriction against slang. You may not want it used in your family, but you should make it clear that this is a family restriction and not a biblical one.

Vulgar words are street language for body functions and body parts. When your child gives you the street word, relate it to the appropriate conventional word. For example, if your daughter comes home with a street word for female genitals and wants to know what it means, simply respond, "Honey, nice boys and girls call that a vagina." If your son asks you the meaning of a street word for male genitals, tell him, "That's what nice boys and girls call a penis." When your child hears someone use the term *son of a bitch* and wants to know what it means, explain to him, "It means your mother is a dog, because a bitch is a female dog. That is why you should never say that to anyone."

Of course, most parents panic when children want to know the meaning of the "F" word. Again, it is important to respond in a way that will not make your child sorry he asked you. After all, you want him to look to you as the primary source of his information about sex. So, tell him, "That's the dirty way to talk about intercourse." If you haven't explained intercourse to him, then you might say, "That's the dirty way to talk about a man and woman making love."

Explain to your children, "Your language is what gives other people their impression of you. So, don't use vulgar or dirty words. If you do, people will think you are naughty and parents of nice boys and girls won't let them play with you."

Profanity is the secular use of sacred words. Make sure your children understand that words like God, Jesus, and Christ are to be used only for talking to and about God. A person who uses these words to express anger, frustration, and surprise empties them of any divine meaning. That is why the Bible prohibits taking God's name in vain. God doesn't want these special words to lose their meaning for you.

Blasphemy is showing contempt for, or making fun of, God. To do this a person's spiritual sensitivities have to be dead. That's why it won't be necesary to talk to your children about it. However, it is good for you to be clear on the subject since you will meet other adults who are confused. It is obvious that no spiritually sensitive person is guilty of blasphemy.

Choices and Priorities

As soon as your child is old enough to make choices, define his options for him and let him choose. Learn to say things like:

"You may have a vanilla, chocolate, or strawberry ice cream cone."

"Do you want to go with your dad and play with Bob, or stay home with me and play with John?"

"Your pink and yellow dresses are ready. Which one do you want to wear?"

"You can have a sundae or a toy; which will it be?"

Training your child to make choices like these prepares him for learning to think in priorities. Among his activities there will always be those of lesser importance and greater importance. At first, you will have to determine those priorities for him, but as soon as he begins to display some ability of his own in this area shift the responsibility more toward him.

Praise him for wise priorities. Explain why his unwise choices were not in his best interests. Help him to anticipate the future consequences for each of his options before he chooses one. Actually, you are teaching him to live by the spiritual law of sowing and reaping (Galatians 6:7–9). With this kind of foundation laid in his childhood character your youngster has taken a giant step toward readiness to face the more complex moral issues of adolescence.

Having helped him determine the quality of his life, let us now consider ways to help him discover how he can best make a living. *Help in vocational direction* is the subject for our next chapter.

Ten
Helping Your Child Find God's Vocational Will

———◆◆———

Have you ever watched small children pretend they were grown-ups going to work? Believe it or not, they are beginning to reflect God's will for their future. God created man to work (Genesis 2:15). In fact, the first day of his life Adam was given a job to do. God put him in the garden and gave him the responsibility of dressing it and keeping it.

Work is not a part of the curse! Long before the fall, Adam had a job. Our need to work is part of God's likeness in us. Jesus said, "My Father worketh hitherto, and I work" (John 5:17).

One of the most valuable gifts you can give your son or daughter is a positive attitude toward work. Maria Montessori concluded that since much of a child's life is spent doing what is called work, every effort should be made to teach the child that work can be enjoyable.

If a young child learns to identify work as the non-fun activity of life, then much of his life is going to be consumed by something he doesn't consider enjoyable. So, in Montessori schools boys and girls learn that work can be fun. Montessori children never call their interaction with learning materials *play*. They call it *work*. They work with clay. They work with blocks. They work with numbers. They work with colors. They work with pitchers and water. And—they find it fun! That's part of the beauty of this approach to education. The child discovers it's fun to work!

God Wants Your Child's Work To Be Fun and Fulfilling

If you enjoy what you do for a living, consider yourself blessed. Most working people don't. That's the result of not discovering their vocational gifts early enough in life. It's important that you help your son or daughter make this discovery as early as possible.

Begin when you see them playing one of children's favorite games—"What I'm Going To Be When I Grow Up." Children start trying on adult roles very early in life. When our grandson was just barely old enough to toddle around the house he would get his dad's tools and pretend he was working.

At first, boys tend to identify with occupations that make a noise. They hear a siren. They see a car. Someone says it is a police car; so, they want the kind of toys that will help them play "policeman." The next time they hear a siren it may be a fire truck. Then, they want toys that will help them play "fireman." Preschool girls still like to play "house" with dolls and furniture.

God's Gifts Are Evident Early in Life

Begin early to help your children discover the needs in His world God has equipped them to meet. Few people see God's will as something so practical. Admittedly, there is a mystical as well as a practical side to God's will for your life. Many aspects of our walk with the Lord will remain a mystery. For example, I'll never know why He included you and me in His grace, but I'm glad He did. However, when it comes to finding God's will for my life's work, He makes no secret of it. It is not a mystery. That discovery is made through a very practical procedure.

Paul makes this clear in Romans 12:1–8: "I beseech you therefore, brethren, by the mercies of God, that ye present your bodies a living sacrifice, holy, acceptable unto God, which is your reasonable service. And be not conformed to this world, but be ye transformed by the renewing of your mind, that ye may prove what is that good, and acceptable, and perfect, will of God.

"For I say, through the grace given unto me, to every man that is among you, not to think of himself more highly than he ought to think, but to think soberly, according as God hath dealt to every man the measure of faith. For as we have many members in one body, and all members have not the same office, so we, being many, are one body in Christ, and every one members one of another.

"Having then gifts differing according to the grace that is given to us, whether prophecy, let us prophesy according to the proportion of faith; or ministry, let us wait on our ministering; or he that teacheth, on teaching; or he that exhorteth, on exhortation; he that giveth, let him do it with simplicity; he that ruleth, with diligence; he that showeth mercy, with cheerfulness."

How is a person to know which of these service gifts are his? The skills identifying them grow out of a child's interaction with his environment and are evident early in his life. With help, these skills can be discovered by trial and error.

Paul makes this very plain. You "prove" God's will by testing your gifts and talents. The future may hide the "where" and "when" of your child's career, but he can discover the "what" by gradually defining gifts and skills through experimentation.

God Calls Each of His Children to a Job

Unfortunately, as a child growing up in the church, I got the impression that if I wasn't called to be a preacher, God didn't care what I did for a living. Great effort was made to motivate young people for the ministry and the mission field, but I can't recall any other vocational future being seen as directly related to God's call on a person's life.

It is important to present the challenge of the ministry to young people. Those called to be ministers and missionaries are special gifts of Christ to the church (Ephesians 4:7–16). However, this does not lessen the importance of a person's vocational call into some other field.

As I have grown older, I understand that it was not the church's intention to deprive those young people who did not feel "called into the ministry" of a sense of divine mission in their work. Yet, I can't help but wonder how different the future might have been for many of my young friends if the church had challenged them to identify God's call on their lives into other vocations by discovering and developing their vocational gifts. After all, the gospel extends God's highest call to each of us. What higher vocation can a person have than to be a member of Christ's body, the church. However, once a person is in the body of Christ, he is challenged to discover God's vocational call through the talents and skills God has given him.

God's Call Dignifies Our Work

Each Christian needs to see his work as God's call on his life. Romans 8:14 reminds us, "For as many as are led by the Spirit of God, they are the sons of God." Feeling that God has gifted me for the job I have and has led me to it, dignifies that work as God's will for me. Without feeling led of God, I certainly wouldn't want to be a minister or missionary. But neither would I want to be a teacher, if God had not called me to the classroom. Or a television technician, if God had not gifted me to serve Him in that way. I certainly wouldn't want to stand on an assembly line and handle the same parts day after day unless I saw that factory as my mission field—the place God had called me to be a witness for Him.

The dignity God's call brings to our work is humorously portrayed in the story of a young man who was hoeing his father's cornfield. It was a hot July day! Anyone who has hoed corn knows that few jobs are harder. Still, there this boy was, perspiration pouring through his overalls, whistling while he worked. He had a big red polka-dotted handkerchief wrapped around his forehead for a sweatband. It was dripping wet. Yet, in spite of how hard he was working, he was happy!

This so mystified a passerby that he couldn't let what he saw and heard go without comment. "Son, don't you know what you're doin' is hard work?" he said, as he motioned for the young man to come closer to the road.

"Yes, sir," the boy replied, leaning his hoe on his chest as he showed the man the callouses on his hands.

"Well," the stranger continued, "the way you're whistlin', a person would think you were enjoyin' what you're doin'."

"I am," the young man reassured him. The conversation continued.

"If what you're doin' is such hard work, how can you enjoy it so much?"

To that the boy concluded, "I guess I forget how hard I'm workin' because I figure I'm doin' somethin' even good God Almighty couldn't do unless I was helpin' Him!"

That's the way God wants each of His children to feel about their work. It is that divine sense of giftedness and dignity you can help your child eventually bring to his work.

Stimulate Your Child's Curiosity About People's Work

Take advantage of your preschooler's fantasy. Expose him to people with a wide variety of occupations and encourage him to ask questions. After he has been with people, ask him questions like, "What do you think of the kind of work he does?" "How interesting do you think it would be?" "Do you think you would like to do something like that?" "Why?" "Why not?"

As soon as it is possible, take him into the place where you work. Let him see what you do. Even though he almost exhausts you with his questions, patiently answer them.

Teach him to be curious when you have guests around. You can help him manage this without being rude. Most people enjoy talking about their work. They will welcome such questions as, "How long have you been doing what you are doing?" "Do you like it?" "What do you like most about it?" "How long do you have to go to school to do what you do?" Feed your child's curiosity about the adult work world. That's where he's headed!

Discover Your Child's Abilities!

Once teacher evaluations begin to be made, notice where your child's strengths lie. Encourage him in the areas where he is most talented. Praise his accomplishments.

If he is verbally or mathematically talented, suggest the possibility of his going to college. Even though he is just eight or nine years old, start planting the idea in his mind. If his skills are in his hands, expose him to a variety of mechanical, technical, and artistic occupations. If he is musical, give him opportunities to develop his talent—but be sure the interest and motivation are his. Attempts to live out our ambitions through our children are most likely to end in failure for them and disappointment for us.

Seven Biblical Occupational Gifts

In the passage quoted earlier in this chapter, Paul provides general descriptions of seven occupational gifts God has given people. Three of them are verbal gifts: teaching, prophecy, and exhortation. Two are related to business: giving and ruling. And two refer to service gifts: ministering and showing mercy.

In Romans 12:1–8, Paul seems to be saying that God gives one or more of these gifts to everyone. He stresses the importance of being realistic in defining our gifts and warns us of the frustration which results when we aren't.

The fact that a person is not choosing to serve God does not alter the divine origin of his talent. James reminds us, "Every good gift and every perfect gift is from above, and cometh down from the Father of lights, with whom is no variableness, neither shadow of turning" (James 1:17).

By becoming aware of these general areas of giftedness, you can provide opportunities for your child to prove himself in one or more of them. For example . . .

1. *Teaching* Expose your child to good books. Encourage him to get a library card and to use it regularly. Notice whether or not he is naturally inclined toward reading. If teaching is a person's gift, he will learn to enjoy reading and studying. Paul implies this when he makes studying a requirement for anyone who is called to teach God's Word. "Study to show thyself approved unto God, a workman that needeth not to be ashamed, rightly dividing the word of truth" (2 Timothy 2:15).

2. *Prophecy* This gift taps the intuitive abilities of the mind. I associate art, poetry, and music with prophetic gifts. People with these talents often march to the tune of another drummer. They lead very active fantasy lives. They are unusually creative. Usually, they don't have great needs to be close to people. This is what enables them to be so confrontive in the expression of their gifts.

Incidentally, a child who is musically gifted will often indicate this to observing parents during his language acquisition years. After all, he is already learning pitch and rhythm in acquiring his language. Notice any special interest he displays in music he hears on the radio, or records he plays on his record player. Observe his fascination for those he's around who are practicing on some musical instrument. Does he approach instruments in an attempt to experiment on his own?

Such musical possibilities in your child don't necessarily mean a career in music awaits him, but they are an indication that he probably will be able to enjoy music as an avocation.

Give him the opportunity to discover his talent and test his commitment. Then the role music will play in his future will define itself.

3. *Exhortation* In the church, exhorters are our cheerleaders. They motivate people with words. They may never overpower you with their content, but they can certainly inspire you with what they have to say.

People with verbal skills like this often make effective salesmen. Preachers, lawyers, and politicians also find these skills helpful in the art of persuading people. If your child is an enthusiast and can motivate his friends to adopt his ideas, he is demonstrating some basic sales skills. These abilities are obvious by the time he starts to school.

4. *Giving* When Paul talks about the gift of giving, he is not talking about tithing. He is referring to those who have been gifted in ways of making money so they can enjoy a ministry of becoming a major source of funding for God's work.

Enterprising abilities can be seen very early in your child's life. Lemonade stands, neighborhood shows, candy and cookie sales—these are some of the early interests of children who may be gifted in finance. A little later, such a youngster may have a paper route or a lawn mowing business. If your child engages in projects like these, how successful is he? How well does he manage money he earns? Can he make a profit from a small investment? Is his business judgment advanced for his age? Does he have the courage to risk?

God cannot trust many people with money. It is too easy for them to fall in love with it. However, with the Lord as his partner, your child can find an exciting future in business if God has gifted him for a ministry in business.

5. *Ruling* Where would we be without administrators? Children who seem to be developing this gift will have greater needs for order and structure in their lives. Schedules and plans are important to them. They need to have a place for everything and to keep everything in its place. Effective administrators come from the ranks of neat and orderly children. Other hints of this gift lie in the child's ability to organize his

peers into teams for play and to set up ways for a group of his friends to work on the same project. Such a child establishes himself early in life as a "take charge" person.

6. *Ministering* This gift may be expressed in menial ways, but it is also a part of many professions. It consists of serving others—meeting their needs. Architects, accountants, book-keepers, librarians, professional consultants—these are some of the more sophisticated forms of ministering. Others who engage in this basic task are: clerks, waiters and waitresses, chefs, short-order cooks, mechanics, technicians, and those who work in the building trades.

Hints of this gift can be seen often in a child's willingness to do things for others. That is, he demonstrates a strong need to be needed.

7. *Showing Mercy* This is an essential gift for anyone in such helping professions as medicine, psychology, and the clergy. It is expressed in the ability to have compassion on those in pain or in some kind of difficulty. Often, children with this inclination have a need to take up for the underdog. Their compassion may also be seen in a tendency to nurse back to health any sick animal they have found.

Guide—Don't Drive!

Paul never intended for these gifts to be interpreted in rigid and dogmatic terms. They were given as guides for helping believers define, through trial and error, the most satisfying and productive ways they can serve God and man.

However, the fact that Paul mentions them underscores the importance of vocational fulfillment to our happiness. If your child is not encouraged to define the direction of his vocational future he is likely to drift into any available job that can provide him enough money to support himself. In that event, he is likely to choose his mate before he discovers any specific job preference. However, once a mate and children are part of his life it will be difficult, if not impossible, for him to acquire the necessary education or training to reach his vocational potential.

That's why it is important for you to begin raising his awareness of his vocational gifts as early in his life as possible. Help him relate his job future to God's call on his life. Teach him to dignify his place of employment with a sense of mission—God wants to use his life there to bless others.

Assess your child's interests and abilities as realistically as possible. Remember, Paul advises all of us ". . . not to think of himself more highly than he ought to think, but to think soberly . . ." (Romans 12:3). Don't be overly ambitious for your child. However, be sure he is aware of the full limits of his potential.

Here are some questions to help you get a realistic picture of your child's job future. *How verbally bright is my child? What kind of grades does he bring home from school? Is he good in English? What about math? Does he like shop or design? Is he mechanically gifted? Is he a people person, or is he more task-oriented?*

Once you have a general understanding of your child's interests and abilities, provide him with opportunities for enrichment. Be patient with him as he sorts it all out. Your job is to keep him aware of the need for vocational direction in his life. It is his responsibility to define that direction for himself. Guide him—don't drive him!

Some youngsters know very early in life what they are going to be. Long before they reach junior high school they have decided to be a doctor, a nurse, a teacher, a truck driver, a mechanic, a computer specialist, an architect, a farmer. However, if your children know that they are headed for college, technical school, or into some kind of apprenticeship training by the time they enter junior high school, be satisfied with that.

In the meantime, expose them to a variety of occupations. You can relate this search to their spiritual growth by making them curious about how many different occupations they can find in the Bible. For starters mention Zenas, the lawyer; Luke, the physician; Lydia, the Christian businesswoman; Aquila and Priscilla, tentmakers; Zaccheus, a government agent; and Joseph, prime minister of Egypt.

As each of your children identifies God's vocational call, prepares himself for it, and pursues it, he will feel like the kid in the cornfield on that hot July day. He will have the joy of knowing he is doing what God has chosen not to do without him. And you will have the joy of knowing you helped him make that discovery!

Eleven
Parenting Through Adoption

———◆———

The home study had been done. All the legal papers had been signed. This was the day Bob and Ethel had looked forward to for months. They were coming to pick up Josh, their newly adopted five-year-old son.

It had been over a year since they started the adoption process. You can imagine their excitement as they approached the agency which had been home for Josh since his parents were killed in a tragic auto accident two years earlier.

Mrs. Howard, the director of the agency, greeted them and ushered them upstairs where Josh was playing with his friends.

Josh had spent many weekends with Bob and Ethel and had always seemed to enjoy himself. So, they thought he would be as anxious to go home with them permanently as they were to take him. However, to their surprise, he turned away from them and clung to his friends. They never dreamed Josh would refuse to go home with them.

Immediately, they began to promise him everything they thought any boy his age would want. "We'll buy you a brand new two-wheeler," Bob bargained. "And we'll get you a new ball glove," Ethel volunteered.

But Josh was unmoved by these bribes. So, Bob and Ethel retreated to Mrs. Howard's office for some advice.

"We have a problem," Bob acknowledged. "Josh doesn't want to leave his friends and go home with us today." "And we've promised him everything," Ethel chimed in. "Even a new bike and glove."

"Have you thought of asking him what he might like to have?" Mrs. Howard wisely inquired.

"No. No, I don't think we have," Bob haltingly admitted.

"Well, why don't you?" she asked.

For the first time, he and Ethel became aware of how one-sided their view of the adoption had been. Remember, a child's feelings and thoughts are a part of the adoption process, too. It's important for you to be in touch with their point of view.

When Bob and Ethel made their way back upstairs they found Josh still playing. He stopped as soon as he saw them and slowly approached.

"Josh, honey," Ethel began, "we just remembered that we never asked you what you might want from us. If you could ask daddy Bob and I for the thing you want more than anything else in the world, what would it be?" Josh stared out into space for a moment and finally asked, "Could you love a fellow?"

Tears filled their eyes as Bob and Ethel responded by throwing their arms around Josh and hugging him so tightly that he could never doubt they loved him. As they left the agency with Josh walking between them hand-in-hand, Bob and Ethel were overwhelmed with emotion. They knew how near they had come to misunderstanding what every child wants and needs more than anything else in the world—his parents' love.

Adoption Is Special!

Although the general principles of parenthood we have taught in this book apply to all children—those who have been adopted as well as natural children—there is something special about the relationship between adopted children and their parents.

After all, adoption is a very special way of having children. However, it is certainly not foreign to the Bible. In fact, all of God's children, but Jesus, are His by adoption.

God had only one "begotten" Son. Because God loved us enough to give His "only begotten Son" for our salvation, we can be His children by adoption. "For ye have not received the spirit of bondage again to fear; but ye have received the Spirit of adoption, whereby we cry, Abba, Father" (Romans 8:15).

There are thousands of homeless babies and children in this world. When your heart is big enough to adopt one of these children and love them as your very own, you will be richly rewarded.

However, the question of why you want to adopt needs to be faced honestly before you are ready for adoption.

1. *Are You Married and Childless?* If so, do you know why you are unable to have children? Before you adopt, it is important for you to know why you are childless.

The ability to conceive children is so deeply rooted in our concepts of manhood and womanhood that some couples find it difficult to submit themselves to the medical tests necessary to determine if some degree of sterility or infertility is involved.

Most couples would prefer to have their own children rather than to adopt; and, the medical technology now exists to make that possible for many. That is why it is so important for you to consult with professionals at a fertility center before concluding it is impossible for you to be a biological parent.

With some professional and technical assistance you may be able to conceive a child. If so, at that point you might want to reconsider your desire to adopt a child. If you discover that it is not possible for you to become natural parents, then you can continue the adoption proceedings with even greater confidence in your decision.

2. *Are You Wanting To Become a Single Parent by Adoption?* Before pursuing this option it is important to explore your intention to *remain* single. If you expect to be married eventually, several issues would seem to question the wisdom of adopting a child while you are single. Let me mention just two.

First, there is no way to be sure your adopted child and your future mate will relate to each other in positive ways. Don't expect them to be compatible immediately and love each other as much as you love each of them.

Second, if you marry and the two of you have your own child, what impact would that have on your adopted child? As natural parents, would your feelings change toward your adopted child?

3. *Are You Motivated To Adopt by Your Compassion for Homeless Children?* This is an admirable quality, but it is not a sufficient reason to adopt a child. Such compassion tends to encourage adoptive parents to build unrealistic expectations of gratitude from the child. Often these leave the child feeling that he is never quite thankful enough that they adopted him. And, the parents are often left feeling unappreciated.

4. *Are You Fearful of the Birth Process?* Some women are so terrified of this experience they would rather adopt their children than to conceive them naturally. However, gynecologists and obstetricians are almost always able to help a woman resolve these fears.

If a man has been exposed to the rare tragedy of a woman dying as a result of childbirth, he may be fearful of allowing his wife to assume that risk. I can understand that. My birth caused my mother's death. As a result, my father became very uncomfortable around pregnant women.

Knowing the tragedy this brought to his life made me unusually anxious during the births of our children. I feared losing my wife. When our grandchildren were born I was more anxious than their fathers were.

If fear of childbirth is a major factor in your decision to adopt, determine to overcome it. Once this is behind you, you may want to give birth to your own child. If you should proceed to adopt, you won't be as likely to second-guess your decision.

Some Things To Remember!

1. *When You Adopt a Child He Brings with Him the Genetic Characteristics of His Parents and Their Families.* He also comes with the accumulated impact his previous environment has made upon him.

Since adoptive parents know the physiological characteristics of their child before they adopt him, they take less of a genetic risk in becoming parents than do natural parents. However, the environmental risks are greater. They usually know little about the youngster's preadoptive environment. Therefore, generally speaking, the younger the child is when you adopt him, the less risk you take and the more control you have over the environmental influences on his life.

These risks are to be taken into account *before* you adopt the child. Once you have adopted the child, don't waste your time worrying about factors you can no longer control. Focus on your relationship with the child and provide him with the most nurturant environment possible. This will help your child grow out of many, if not most, of the hurts from his past.

2. *If You Adopt Your Child in Infancy, Let Him Grow Up Knowing That He Is Adopted.* As soon as he is old enough to talk, tell him how he came into your family.

You may want to say something like, "Honey, there are two ways a mommy and daddy can have a baby. One way is for mommy and daddy to grow a baby in a special room in mommy's tummy. Another way is for them to fall in love with a baby who grew in the tummy of another mommy who couldn't keep him.

"Every baby comes from a mommy's tummy. But sometimes, the mommy from whose tummy the baby comes can't take care

144

of her baby. So, she gives her baby to another mommy who loves the baby just as much as if he had come from her own tummy. That's how we had you. We chose you. You see, once a baby is in a mommy's tummy *she can't choose any other baby.* She has to take the one who is in her tummy, but *your mommy and daddy chose you. We could have had some other baby, but when we saw you we loved you so much we didn't want any other baby. We wanted you. So, you see, you are very special to us.*"

This is a story you will have to repeat to your child again and again through the years. As he gets older he will have more questions about how he came to live with you. He may want to know why his mother gave him away. If you know, tell him. If you don't, tell him that, too.

Always put his mother in the most favorable position possible. Help him to understand that she loved him enough to want him to have a better home than she could give him. However, you will want to make it clear that she couldn't have loved him any more than you love him. That's how special he is! Help him understand that not very many boys and girls are loved as much as he is.

3. *If You Have Natural Children You Will Need To Explain the Nature of Your Relationship with Each Child in Such a Way That He Knows He Is Special to You.* Be careful not to favor your natural children!

On the other hand, don't discriminate against them in your efforts to be fair to your adopted child. Remember, it is the extremes you need to avoid. Children are very understanding. A mistake once in a while will be quickly forgiven and forgotten. So long as you treat them as much alike as possible most of the time they will have the sense of belonging that is so important to their emotional well being.

4. *When Your Adopted Child Reaches His Teens He May Want To Discover Who His Natural Parents Are.* Remember, this is a normal, natural desire. If you are able to keep this in mind, it will make you feel less rejected and threatened.

Here are some suggestions for helping you manage this difficult time.

Your child is likely to see this search as an attempt to discover his "real" parents. Be sure he understands that *you* are his "real" parents. His biological parents may be referred to as his "natural" parents, but they are not his "real" parents. They gave him life, but you taught him how to live. You parented him.

Your child needs to know that since his natural parents made their decision to give him up for adoption they have built futures for themselves which have not included him. If he succeeds in finding them, his sudden appearance could seriously disrupt their lives.

For example, if his natural parents are now married to other people, it is highly unlikely that their new mates know anything about him. Try to help him realize the problems he could create for their marriages by showing up unannounced. Do your best to prepare him for the rejection *he* is likely to experience.

There is also the strong possibility that his mother or father has had children by their new mate. Can you imagine how disturbing it might be for those children to discover that their mother or dad had another child as a result of his or her involvement with another man or woman?

Point out all these risks. Then, if your child still wants to make the search, don't forbid him to do it. Simply be available to help him deal with the circumstances as they develop. By assuming this attitude you are likely to be more loved than ever once he is through with his search.

Natural Children Pose Problems, Too!

Having alerted you to some of the unique issues facing adoptive parents, I need to remind you that raising natural children has its challenges, too. In our day, any way you choose to parent children has risks. However, the rewards far outweigh the risks.

Those who choose to have children are investing in the happiness of their later years. The future should find them enjoying a harvest of healthy family relationships with their children and grandchildren.

Remember, you are giving your adopted child the advantages of a loving and stable home environment. As he grows older and realizes the risks you were willing to assume because of your love for him, he will have his own way of rewarding you.

Twelve
Help!
I'm a Stepparent!

———◆———

    If you think marriage and parenthood are demanding tasks, talk to someone who is trying to put together a stepfamily. More and more adults and children are finding themselves confronted with this challenge. Most of those who succeed reach out to someone for help along the way.

    Jeff and Donna were wise enough to know that. When they took their seats in my office, the tension between them was obvious. Jeff sat as close as he could to the left arm of the couch and Donna sat on the right. After a few strained pleasantries, I asked, "How long have the two of you been married?" "Three months," Donna replied.

    "What kind of problems could land you in an office like mine just three months after your marriage?" I continued. "Oh, it's not us, Doc. It's the children," Jeff volunteered. "You see, both Donna and I have been married before and she has two children by her first husband: Greg, seven, and, Susan, five. These kids thought there was nobody like me when I was dating their mother, but now that we're married—it's a different story."

I urged Jeff to tell me what was happening. "Well, I suppose they're jealous of me or something," he replied.

When I asked him why he felt that way, Jeff responded, "Every time their mother and I are together they want her to do something for them or they want to be with us. And when I try to make them leave us alone, Donna gets upset with me."

At this point I had the general picture, but I needed more detail before I could begin to help Jeff and Donna rescue their relationship from the risky waters of their second matrimonial sea. So they began to tell me their story.

Jeff and his first wife met in church. After going together for about two years, they married. He was 27; she was 25. Three years later, while she was in the early weeks of pregnancy, Jeff's first wife was killed in a tragic auto accident. Even after he recovered from the shock and grief of it all, it was several years before Jeff was ready to think about marriage again.

Jeff and Donna met at the same church where he had found his first wife. Donna was recovering from a very painful divorce. Her first husband had left her and their two children for his secretary—a single woman twelve years younger than Donna. Greg was almost three at that time, and Susan was still breast feeding.

Donna toughed it through the shock of her divorce. Her husband gave her what equity they had in their home and faithfully paid child-support. It was difficult for Donna to consent to the visitation rights he requested, but the court insisted that as long as he was faithful in supporting the children, he was entitled to see them.

Like many Christian mothers, Donna was fearful that her children would be attracted to their father's morally loose ways. She prayed daily that God would send her a Christian husband who would help her form a Christian two-parent family for Greg and Susan. She thought Jeff was the answer to her prayer. So, after going with him for almost three years, she married him.

Three months later, here they were in my office. Nothing seemed to be working out the way they had planned. By this time, it was obvious to me that both of them had entered the marriage with highly unrealistic expectations. My job would be to help them see that and to define realistic goals for their relationship. Although several sessions would be required to work through the emotional issues involved, there was much to be done in this first meeting.

I began by saying, "The two of you have come through some very painful experiences before finding each other. I can understand why it is so important to you that your relationship works out well for you and the children. That's much more likely to happen if you are realistic in what you attempt."

Bury Your Old Dream and Build a New One!

"What do you mean?" Donna asked.

"Well, neither of you can take the place of your spouse's first mate," I replied. "This is a new relationship that will gradually determine its own identity. Donna, you can't be expected to fulfill Jeff's dreams of what marriage might have been like had his first wife lived. And Jeff can't become to you all you wish your first husband had been.

"You may find yourselves wishing that you could start your married life as though neither of you had been married before, but that is a fantasy that can only hinder your attempts to succeed in this marriage. The reality is that both of you have been married before and this does affect your relationship with each other. Your ability to see this for what it is can help you make the most of your future together."

Children and New Mates Can Be Jealous of Each Other

"What are some of the ways we can expect our previous marriages to affect us?" Jeff asked.

"Why have you come to see me?" I responded.

"The kids are causing us trouble," he replied.

"That's right," I agreed. "You are having trouble with step-parenting. Since you and your first wife never had any children, you never had a chance to discover the difference children can make in a marriage. Naturally, you expected Donna to put you first in the home, once you were married. In fact, you would be unusual if you weren't feeling a little jealous of the children."

"I'm glad to hear you say that," Jeff replied. "That makes me feel more normal. But I don't want to be jealous of the kids. How can I get over it?"

Children Need To Know It Is Not Their Fault

"Maybe it will help both of you to take a look at the children's side," I suggested. "It's not their fault their father and mother couldn't get along. Donna should be sure they know that. Sometimes children mistakenly assume that had they behaved better their father would not have left them.

"They want to love both of their parents and should be given permission to do that. It's only natural for them to dream of the possibility that their father and mother will get back together again. After all, if you were in their place, wouldn't you be praying this would happen?"

Jeff and Donna both nodded affirmatively. Donna's eyes teared up a little as I continued.

"Greg and Susan need to be told that their father and mother will never be married to each other again. Such finality may seem cruel, but children can deal with *unpleasant certainty* in a more healthy way than they can manage *uncertainty*. However, they need to know that both of their parents still love them very much and that ways will always be made for them to experience that love."

"That's what scares me," Donna interrupted. "I don't like it when their father takes them and his girl friend is with him. The kids see him drink and smoke and do things I don't want my children exposed to."

Your Children Can See the Difference!

"On the other hand," I suggested, "they are his children too, and they will be exposed to those things in their friends' homes even if you could keep them from visiting their father. Parents just can't protect children that much in today's world. However, as they visit their father, they will have the opportunity to observe the difference between his life-style and yours. Can't you believe that over the years they will be able to see that your way of life brings more happiness?"

"I . . . I guess I hadn't seen it that way," Donna admitted.

"And if circumstances were to become too objectionable you could always complain to the court through your lawyer," I offered. "However, give your former husband the benefit of the doubt. Even though he's not a Christian and didn't treat you right as his wife, it's obvious he does love his children. Just because he wasn't a good mate to you doesn't mean he can't be a good father to Greg and Susan."

"I suppose you're right," Donna reluctantly conceded. "However, it does make me feel better to know that if the kids come home with stories which are too wild there is something I can do about it."

"While we're talking about the children's side," I continued, "try to remember that they have had their mother all to themselves for the past few years. Jeff, it's too much to expect children this young to give up first place in their mother's life without a struggle."

"Yeah, I can see that," Jeff agreed. "I guess this is another way our previous marriages are affecting us. I never had any competition from children in my first marriage and I guess I didn't expect any in this one." I then proceeded to give Jeff and Donna some standard information we share with couples who bring into their marriage children from former marriages.

Boy friend vs. Stepparent

Children have a way of loving mother's boy friends and despising stepparents. To the onlooker, the reasons are obvious. Boy friends take children special places and buy them things. Much of this stops after the marriage. Seldom, if ever, do boy friends attempt to discipline mother's children. However, once married, the stepfather often sees the children take advantage of their mother. He insists that she is spoiling them rotten and should be harsher in the punishments she administers to them.

This, of course, understandably endears him to the children . . . actually, it does just the opposite. The children then seek protection from the stern stepfather by appealing to their mother. She extends herself to the children, obviously disagreeing with the stepfather's assessment of the situation. This angers him. His stance with the children becomes even more severe. This cycle continues, driving mother and children closer together and husband and wife farther apart.

Let the Children Come First for a While

How can a couple avoid this? The husband of a woman with children from a previous marriage should assume that during the early months of their marriage the woman's children will be closer to her than he will be. After all, this woman was married to another man who promised to stay with her for life and where is he? She knows she has a lifelong relationship with her children . . . and she hopes her new husband will be with her that long, but she can't be sure yet.

As the marriage assumes permanency, it will be easier for the wife to put a little more distance between herself and her children. Then her husband can assume the place he needs and should have in her life. Until then, he is wise to patiently love his wife and support her efforts to discipline her children.

153

A New Husband Is Not Necessarily a New Daddy

Often, a woman seeks in her second husband a new "daddy" for her children. However, no man can take the place of their biological father. The older the children are, the more impractical it is for a stepfather to attempt it.

He *can* be the children's friend, and he *should* be. This is a realistic goal. And he should be supportive of his wife in her discipline of the children.

In instances where the children are young enough, a stepfather's love over a period of years may earn him a disciplinary role in their lives. This can only be effective as the children give him the role. If he assumes it, the antagonism between him and the children will intensify.

Natural Children Complicate the Process

"No wonder we are having problems," Donna said. "I really thought Jeff could become a Christian father to my children. Now I can see how impractical that is. And what if Jeff and I want children of our own? After all, he deserves that right."

"Well, Donna," I responded, "that will complicate your relationship, but if the two of you want other children you should be able to manage it. After all, the important thing is to see that each child is loved and disciplined in keeping with the uniqueness of his disposition.

"Or course, you will have to see that you are not prejudiced in favor of the children who are the product of your love. This will probably be more difficult for Jeff than for you, since all of the children will be yours.

Give Grandparents a Chance

"Let me cover one more area before we end the session today," I finally said. "How do Greg and Susan get along with their father's parents?"

"Very well," Donna replied, "and I have wondered what we should do about the relationship, because Jeff's parents want to take an interest in the children, too."

"Why not let them enjoy both sets of grandparents?" I suggested. "They are more likely to be open to a relationship with Jeff's parents if they aren't forced to give up seeing their paternal grandparents." Jeff agreed.

"Well, how do you feel after your first visit?" I asked.

"I guess my feelings are mixed," Donna volunteered. "I can see we were going about things in the wrong way. I think I have a much more realistic view of our situation, but it is more complicated than I had ever imagined. It's not just a matter of your new husband taking the place of your first one and becoming a new daddy to your children." "Yeah, it's a lot more complicated than I thought, too," Jeff chimed in, "but understanding it better makes me feel more confident that with the Lord's help we can make it work."

I saw Jeff and Donna several more times. During those sessions we covered other unique characteristics of the stepfamily. Here are a few of them.

1. *Stepfamily Relationships Proceed Through Stages.* Most stepfamilies go through three stages in their efforts to get along with each other. For the first few weeks everyone is hopeful and happy. They want things to go well.

Soon after that, conflicts and confrontations begin to break in on the scene. Usually, these are tolerated for several months.

Finally, as the tension mounts, conflicts become more frequent and more intense. Now, the relationships are in a crisis stage. It usually requires about two years for the average stepfamily to work through this crisis period. Children in their middle years seem to have more difficulty coping with this stage than preschoolers or teenagers. Sometimes the anger they feel toward the parent who has left the family tends to be directed toward the stepparent.

It may help you to see the experience of stepparenting as being somewhat like an organ transplant. A new parent, like a new liver, may be what the body needs to be healthy. However, a critical period follows after surgery, when the body may attempt to reject it. In the crisis stage of the stepfamily, children may attempt to reject a stepparent, hoping to defeat the marriage and have their natural parent all to themselves again. Mates must be prepared to patiently negotiate their way through this challenge.

2. *Parenting Tends To Take Precedence Over Marriage*
Keeping your marriage in focus is difficult when you are stepparents. It is easy to concentrate your attention on conflicts among the children or between them and their stepparent. However, it is more important for the entire family that you work on your marriage bond. As your marriage becomes healthier and the love bond between you and your mate grows stronger, it will provide you the flexibility you need to cooperatively resolve your differences over how the children should be raised. During your negotiations try to define new ways of loving, disciplining, working, rewarding, and playing that are acceptable to both of you.

3. *Stepparents Tend To Catastrophize Common Problems* Remember, if your children were being raised in a family with both of their natural parents they would still have many of the same problems you are concerned about. Before you panic, stop long enough to ask yourself, "Is this problem unique to our stepfamily?" In most cases, the answer will be no. Then, breathe a sigh of relief and approach it like any other parent would.

Jeff and Donna found it helpful to be made aware of these things. I'm glad to tell you things have worked out beautifully for them. But, remember, they didn't wait until their marriage was a wreck before they sought help. They were wise enough to know they needed driving lessons.

Excellent information for those attempting to form stepfamilies is available from the *Stepfamily Association of America Inc., 28 Allegheny Avenue, Suite 1307, Baltimore, Maryland 21204.*

Being a stepparent isn't easy. Neither is living with one. Yet, most things that are worth having in life are worth working for.

Bibliography

For those who desire more information and counsel on nurturing the young child, the author suggests that the following books may prove particularly helpful:

Braga, Joseph and Braga, Laurie. *Children and Adults: Activities for Growing Together.* Englewood Cliffs, N.J.: Prentice-Hall, 1976.

Changler, Caroline; Lourie, Reginald; Peters, Anne DeHuff. Edited by Laura Dittman. *Early Child Care: the New Perspectives.* New York: Atherton Press, 1968.

Chess, Stella, M.D.; Thomas, Alexander, M.D.; Birch, Herbert G., M.D., Ph.D. *Your Child Is a Person: a Psychological Approach to Parenthood Without Guilt.* New York: Penguin, 1977.

Colarusso, Calvin A., M.D.; Nemiroff, Robert A., M.D. *Adult Development: a New Dimension in Psychodynamic Theory and Practice.* New York: Plenum Pub., 1981.

Curran, Dolores. *Traits of a Healthy Family.* Minneapolis: Winston Press, 1983.

Dinkmeyer, Don. C. *Child Development: the Emerging Self.* Englewood Cliffs, N.J.: Prentice-Hall, 1965.

Dorr, Darwin; Zax, Melvin; Bonner, Jack W., III, ed. *The Psychology of Discipline.* New York: International Universities Press, 1983.

Frank, Jerome D. *Persuasion and Healing: a Comparative Study of Psychotherapy.* 2d rev. ed. New York: Schocken, 1974.

Ginott, Haim. *Between Parent and Child.* New York: Avon, 1969.

Kagan, Jerome. *The Growth of the Child: Reflections on Human Development.* New York: W. W. Norton, 1978.

Kastenbaum, Robert. *Growing Old: Years of Fulfillment.* New York: Harper & Row, 1979.

Lamb, Michael E., ed. *The Role of the Father in Child Development.* New York: John Wiley & Sons, 1976.

Montagu, Ashley. *Touching: the Human Significance of the Skin.* New York: Columbia University Press, 1971.

Mussen, Paul H., ed. *Carmichael's Manual of Child Psychology.* (3rd ed., vol. 1) New York: John Wiley & Sons, 1970.

The Study Group of New York (Berges, Emily Trafford, et al.). *Children and Sex: the Parents Speak.* New York: Facts on File, 1983.

Wheat, Ed., M.D., and Wheat, Gaye. *Intended for Pleasure.* Old Tappan, N.J.: Fleming H. Revell, 1977.

The author has a five-part film series on emotions and a thirteen-part video series on parenthood training. For information on how to order either series, call Emerge Ministries, 800/621-5207; in Ohio, call 216/867-5603.